T0029793

"Leading as a team used to be a novelty; now ministries are going to thrive in a rapidly chan laborative team that can weather the storms provide a step-by-step guide to take an inventory of our souls, assess our situations, and build a team that matches the challenges of this cultural moment. Filled with actionable best practices, this is a road map to team resilience."

Glenn Packiam, lead pastor at Rockharbor Church and senior fellow at the Barna Group

"Leaders help organizations grow not through their own brilliance but by developing unstoppable teams. In *The Resilience Factor*, Ryan, Léonce, and Warren bring expert advice together to provide a clear road map for Christian leaders. Use these steps to help your team move forward to influence lasting, positive change."

Dave Stachowiak, host of the *Coaching for Leaders* podcast

"This book is an incredibly important read for the corporate, relational, and emotional fragility so many of us around the world are experiencing. Resilience is the only path forward."

Heather Thompson Day, author of *It's Not Your Turn* and associate professor of communication at Andrews University

"Many of us know we need to be more resilient—but how do we get there? *The Resilience Factor* artfully explains the new leadership realities of our day and expertly guides us step-by-step to become the resilient leaders and teams needed for tomorrow. I'll be taking my teams through this insightful workbook, and I highly encourage everyone do the same!"

Kadi Cole, leadership consultant and author of *Developing Female Leaders*

"Building a healthy and thriving team is essential to achieving your mission. *The Resilience Factor* is one of the most practical and helpful books I've read on the subject of teams! The authors break down the fundamentals of resilient teams with actionable exercises and thoughtful discussion questions that will equip you to not just dream of building an unbreakable team but actually take action to become one."

Jenni Catron, leadership and culture coach and founder and CEO of 4Sight Group

"Rebounding after a setback is the hallmark of a unique and long-lasting team. As we help thousands of churches rebuild their teams post-pandemic, I'm thrilled that Ryan, Léonce, and Warren have built a road map toward resilience. Read this book with your team. You'll see immediate results."

William Vanderbloemen, founder and CEO of Vanderbloemen

"Many leaders struggle to overcome internal culture problems, growing trust deficits, and the loss of team productivity. Thankfully, this influential new book is an instant go-to resource for building an effective team. In addition to helping teams develop clarity of purpose and align around goals, this book will equip and empower leaders to build teams that last."

Craig Groeschel, senior pastor of Life.Church and author of *Lead Like It Matters*

"Léonce has done it again! It's almost as if Léonce and his teammates are your coaches, you are in the locker room of ministry, and they are walking you step-by-step through how to win the game. If you want to upgrade your team and level up your leadership, take time and let this team coach you through this masterful book."

Albert Tate, lead pastor of Fellowship Church and author of *How We Love Matters*

"The recent reset means we're all rookies. And with so many leaders throwing in the towel, this is one of the most practical books to help you assess your situation and pioneer this moment with confidence. It's not a manual for what to do; it's a guide to rediscover the redemptive edge your specific team offers your specific community in this hour of need. No two teams will come out with the same answers, but every single team will finish with a plan of attack."

Grant Skeldon, next gen director at Q Ideas and author of *The Passion Generation*

"Too often, teams are hampered by a lack of focus, internal discord, or complacency. *The Resilience Factor* is a response to these problems. Ryan Hartwig, Léonce Crump Jr., and Warren Bird provide an easy-to-follow framework for addressing common pitfalls, which helps leaders develop teams built on trust, purpose, and accountability. *The Resilience Factor* holds the key for creating teams that can change the world!"

Dave Ferguson, lead visionary of NewThing and author of *BLESS: 5 Everyday Ways to Love Your Neighbor and Change the World*

"If the past decade has taught leaders anything, it's that great teams don't endure against all odds by failing to change. Instead they use setbacks and chaos to grow stronger, resilient, and ready for the future. This book will teach your team exactly how to do that."

David Burkus, author of *Leading from Anywhere* and *Under New Management*

THE
RESILIENCE
FACTOR

A STEP-BY-STEP
GUIDE TO CATALYZE
AN UNBREAKABLE TEAM

RYAN T. | LÉONCE B. | WARREN
HARTWIG | CRUMP JR. | BIRD

FOREWORD BY TOD BOLSINGER

An imprint of InterVarsity Press
Downers Grove, Illinois

InterVarsity Press
P.O. Box 1400 | Downers Grove, IL 60515-1426
ivpress.com | email@ivpress.com

InterVarsity Press® is the publishing division of InterVarsity Christian Fellowship/USA®. For more information, visit intervarsity.org.

Scripture quotations, unless otherwise noted, are from The Holy Bible, English Standard Version, copyright © 2001 by Crossway Bibles, a division of Good News Publishers. Used by permission. All rights reserved.

While any stories in this book are true, some names and identifying information may have been changed to protect the privacy of individuals.

The publisher cannot verify the accuracy or functionality of website URLs used in this book beyond the date of publication.

Cover design: David Fassett

Interior design: Daniel van Loon

ISBN 978-1-5140-0568-2 (print) | ISBN 978-1-5140-0569-9 (digital)

Printed in the United States of America ♾

Library of Congress Cataloging-in-Publication Data
A catalog record for this book is available from the Library of Congress.

30   29   28   27   26   25   24   23 | 12   11   10   9   8   7   6   5   4   3   2   1

CONTENTS

FOREWORD

TOD BOLSINGER

No one will follow you off *the map if they don't trust you* on *the map*. In the wake of and amid the lingering impact of the Covid-19 pandemic, books on resilience became bestsellers. A number of frontline, thoughtful, and experienced leaders entered the resilience conversation offering insight and practical wisdom. For most, the conversation of resilience is connected to *individual* survival—to personal grit.

What does it take for a leader to "bounce back," to "hang in," and to "keep going" when facing daunting odds, disruptive circumstances, or what seems like sure defeat? What does it take for the one calling the shots to endure? Like US Navy SEALs who survive a "hell week" of all-night, days-on-end training in the freezing Pacific Ocean, those with real resilience are those who can stick it out.

But what most leaders don't understand about the SEAL training is that it isn't meant to make you a superhero; it's meant to *make you a team*. The Navy SEALs go through "hell week" not only to weed out the weak but also to teach the strong that they will endure only *if they learn to be trustworthy people who trust each other*.[1]

My favorite definition of resilience comes from Andrew Zolli: "the capacity . . . to maintain . . . core purpose and integrity in the face of dramatically changed circumstances."[2] As one who spends my life writing, speaking, and consulting on change, the word *maintain* doesn't exactly get me out of bed in the morning. I am more energized by verbs like *disrupt*, *innovate*, *trailblaze*, *adapt*, and *explore*. I spend my life helping leaders learn how to go off the map.

But just like the SEALs who need to learn to be people who can be trusted to maintain their core purpose and integrity in times of great stress, leadership teams need to be trained in how to become truly resilient *teams* in order to face the challenges of a disrupted world.

What Ryan Hartwig, Léonce Crump, and Warren Bird offer in *The Resilience Factor: A Step-by-Step Guide to Catalyze an Unbreakable Team* is a kind of intense training for preparing a team to enter into the challenges of the uncharted territory of a dramatically and rapidly changing world with the most preparation and the highest amount of trust possible. They offer an excellent primer of *on*-the-map leadership that develops the trust and character needed to go *off* the map.

What the authors call an *unbreakable team* is one that has both the character and the camaraderie to work together when the challenges are most intense and when the world is most unpredictable.

This book is a training manual. But even more than that, it is a *team* training manual. Because in the final analysis, this *team* of authors both write and model for us that the answer is *each other*.

WHY YOU NEED THE RESILIENCE FACTOR

You probably saw the heart-wrenching photos in the news, and maybe even said a prayer. On November 8, 2018, a massive forest fire, whipped by fifty-mile-an-hour winds, virtually razed the town of Paradise, California.

When the devastation ended, the town of twenty-seven thousand people was nearly erased. Thirteen thousand homes and many businesses —some 85 percent of the town's structures—had vanished in a few minutes. Abandoned cars melted down to their axles as people fled.

Worse, not only did this most destructive wildfire in California's recent history destroy structures, but it also obliterated a once tight-knit community of families, friends, neighborhoods, schools, businesses, and churches. In the months that followed, people fought to put their lives—and community—back together. Many had to find new homes, new jobs, new schools, and new relationships. Ultimately, a new normal.

You might think that in the wake of such devastation, the survivors would have simply waved the white flag and given up completely on the place they once called home.

Many did, but not Paradise Alliance Church. They did just the opposite. The church chose to strategically partner in rebuilding a new community. Their teams rose to the challenge of the hour, reaching a level of resilience that enabled significant community service while transforming each team member.

Josh Gallagher, the lead pastor of the church, reported, "Some people within our staff and leadership teams wanted us to focus primarily on the people in our congregation. Instead, we decided that this was God's moment for us to demonstrate to the community that 'you are loved'— the catchphrase we use for our church."

This was not an easy shift, as each staff member had been personally affected by trauma and loss. Nor was it a comfortable shift. "Every single team member who chose to stay had to adapt a new paradigm for what it means to be on their team," Josh said. "In the end, the people that thrived—the ones who were the most resilient—were those who realized that they had to transition both in how we think about our roles and our ministry, and also in being willing to be okay with so much unknown ahead."

But not everyone thrived in this new normal. Some team members could not or chose not to embrace the changes. "I took it personally when one of my team members walked away from what God was doing," Josh said, "but I eventually realized that the group could still become healthier and better without certain people on the team. Ultimately, I decided that when God removes a team member, it is to raise up new members."

Everyone who remained was willing to say, "I'll do whatever needs to be done for the sake of the church and our community." That meant adjusting people's roles, the church budget, and how they executed team meetings—as well as how they served the community.

For example, many relief centers popped up in the aftermath of the fire, but no place existed for the community itself to gather. So the church started a Thursday-night dinner, feeding people a high-quality meal and providing a chance for the community to come together. "At its height we were serving one thousand meals a week," Josh said.

As the first anniversary of the fire approached, anticipating that people would want to reflect, the church put on an event that drew five thousand people—a sizable percentage of those who had remained or were beginning to return. "We wanted to be the center of hope for the community. We wanted to convey, 'There's still hope here. God has a plan for you,'" Josh explained. Each year since then, the church has done something on that fateful anniversary.

"We arrived at this point only because God allowed us to reimagine ourselves as a team," Josh summarized. "I had no idea that such resilience could come from so many people—but God did. Today we are a team that through him can face *anything*. Plus, our reputation in the community has changed for the better. We are known today as the 'You-Are-Loved Church.'"

Despite the circumstances before them, and despite the hardships they faced, the teams at Paradise Alliance Church chose to allow the experience to strengthen their resolve, learn from the chaos, define and accomplish new goals, and experience the deep satisfaction that only endurance can produce. These were resilient people who formed resilient teams that faced—with excellence—even the most oppressive set of challenges. *They possessed the resilience factor!*

DOES *RESILIENT* DESCRIBE YOU OR YOUR TEAM?

If your church, ministry, or organization is like most others, you've taken some form of a significant hit pretty much every year, with or without a pandemic. But unfortunately, your team probably isn't ready today for what's coming tomorrow.

Like it or not, most teams are just one blow away from chaos, crash, or even collapse. But God has called your team to good work by his enabling, and you have worked too hard for too long for your team to experience a wipeout. You need an advantage. Your team needs the secret weapon many in leadership never saw coming, but wise Christians, psychologists, and sociologists have known about for years. You need the resilience factor!

According to the *Merriam-Webster Dictionary*, resilient people are:

1. able to become strong, healthy, or successful again after something bad happens;

2. able to return to an original shape after being pulled, stretched, pressed, bent, etc.

To walk successfully and confidently into an unknown future, your church, ministry, or organization needs the resilience factor. If a team embodies the kind of resilience we describe in this book, it will grow to be unbreakable, able to face anything while flourishing in the process.

Today's the day to begin the journey of building an unbreakable team for your future. Whether or not your teammates call you the leader of your team, you can play a vital role to spur your team to grow more effective, healthy, and resilient. In the following pages we'll show you how.

THE CONTEXT FOR RESILIENT TEAMS

With the fog of the massive disruptions of the last few years finally clearing, it's prime time for Christian leaders to think, dream, and create a preferred future. And there's no better way to do so than through a flourishing team.

> Management is concerned with maintaining the status quo. But leadership entails envisioning what could be.

But the only way your team will begin to shape the preferred future is by accepting the world as it is rather than pining for what you remember as normal. Of course, disruption is normal, and the relative stability and predictability recent generations have known are *abnormal* (see movement 9).

Reframing your outlook can lead to a bright future. In a world without disruption, leadership is not required. You simply manage what is. But tomorrow's world marked by disruption requires innovation, imagination, and resilience. These are today's marks of leadership.

Many leaders and teams are currently navigating the discomfort of transitioning from management to leadership. Management is concerned with administrating effectively what is, maintaining the status quo. But leadership entails envisioning what could be and then engaging in such a way as to bring that preferred future into reality.[1]

This is our call to your team: Do not settle for longing for the past or even managing what is now. Instead, rise and lead. Embrace the world as it is and lead through it, engaged fully with these new realities before you.

New reality 1: Today's world generally distrusts leadership. Culturally, much of what used to be accepted practice and understood norms for leadership and followership has largely vanished. Often in today's new world,

- Direction is seen as dominance.

- Clarity is equated with control.

- Expectations are viewed as burdens.

- Accountability is called abuse.

Of course, domineering, controlling, abusive leaders do exist (and they should be confronted, corrected, and if necessary, rooted out, for that brand of "leadership" is unacceptable). But the cultural conception of *leadership* itself is now often cast in those categories whether deserved or not. Leaders of the future must recognize the skepticism and altered expectations of those they lead. Resilient teams will provide a healthy context for directive leadership and accountability, with protections offered when that leadership goes awry.

New reality 2: Team leadership is here to stay. Back in the old days (2015) when Ryan and Warren released *Teams That Thrive*, solo leadership paradigms were a dime a dozen, championed by nationally prominent leaders who sought to train individualistic leaders in their image. In the intervening years, when so many leaders imploded either personally, organizationally, or both, their stories have been memorialized in podcasts, the predominant news media of our time. The message of these podcast narratives (such as *The Rise and Fall of Mars Hill*[2]) is leaders' gifts outpaced character and left a pile of dead bodies behind the bus. These leadership collapses spurred a tectonic shift in followers' expectations of those they allow to lead them. More and more, followers expect humility, the willingness to not only acknowledge but also organize based on an understanding of personal weakness, and to focus on personal and relational spiritual health. With these, followers hope they will be protected from the fall of that single leader. They expect leadership to be done by a team—for protection, for health, for trust, and for greater effectiveness.

New reality 3: Your team is largely a new team. The Great Resignation that started in 2021 has transformed—or will transform—the membership of your team. In 2021 alone sixty-nine million Americans quit their jobs—many of them moving away, whether for retirement or to shift to other employment.[3] Your team was likely not immune to this unprecedented shuffle. You likely have said goodbye to trusted (or distrusted) colleagues, and hello to others, who brought new desires and requirements with them.

New reality 4: Your new team comes with new expectations. Indeed, the greatest consequence of the Great Resignation was not team makeup but the Great Reset of employee expectations.[4] Fewer employees willingly put work at the center of their lives; they require their workplaces to be places where they can pursue work that's meaningful to *them* while they balance other desires in life. Team leaders who ignore this new reality will see continual turnover and, more importantly, will bang their heads against the wall when they just can't seem to generate momentum on their given tasks.

> The greatest consequence of the Great Resignation was not team makeup but the Great Reset of employee expectations.

New reality 5: The pandemic may be officially over, but its effects will ripple for years to come. Communication scholars like to talk about the "afterlife of a conversation"—the residue, good, bad, or indifferent, from a conversation that never goes away. Similarly, the residue of the pandemic will never go away. This is no real surprise, but it deserves underlining: those you serve—your church, customers, clients, and constituents—have developed new ways of doing just about everything, whether attending church, engaging in spiritual community, buying goods, or pursuing entertainment. They're never fully going back to prepandemic ways of thinking. These changes are here to stay. For your church or organization to thrive in the future, you must align with this new reality. A resilient team will help you discern and then move toward new markets and new meaning-makers.

New reality 6: The world—and your team—carries new levels of tension and stress. Former Saddleback pastor Rick Warren recently named five huge storms that the world has weathered in the last few years: global infirmity, social instability, racial inequality, financial insecurity, and political incivility. We're sure you've been touched by most if not all of these storms. Though any one of these storms is enough to cause heightened tension and prolonged stress, you have been facing all five at the same time! Your team will be required to lean into the aftermath of these storms, address the very real challenges and tensions experienced in your community and press toward unity in your community.

New reality 7: Everyone's exhausted. Though bright spots shimmer on the horizon, the reality is that your team is tired from the pandemic's long, gradual draining of their reserves. Your team members don't just need to be pushed toward a reenergized mission; they need to be seen and cared for. Look at the statistics across society on stepping back and giving up. At a recent Global Leadership Summit, noted Christian psychologist Henry Cloud shared that diagnosable mental health issues rose from 17 percent to over 40 percent during 2021 and 2022. When you combine that sharp increase in mental diagnoses with extremely high resignation rates, as well as the anecdotal data of burned-out and blown-up leaders across the globe, the picture becomes quite clear: these last few years have worn everyone out.[5] The leaders who see and care for their team—even while pursuing grand efforts—will experience greater impact and lesser turnover, building momentum that drives their organizations into the future.

New reality 8: Too many of today's leaders were trained in yesterday's school of leadership. Remote work is here to stay, more and more people will cobble together their income from a conglomeration of side hustles, and your organizational values will attract or repel more potential staffers than ever before. In this new world of work, most likely what worked to get you *here* won't work to get you *there*.[6] While Jesus and our foundations in Scripture don't change, people's assumptions, perspectives, and cultural context continually change, as do the tools available to us. If you were trained in the old school of teams, it's time to learn in the new school—and that will require you to unlearn some principles and practices that worked for you in the old world, but won't drive success for teams in the new world.

COULD YOUR CURRENT TEAM FACE ANYTHING AND THRIVE?

> *What worked to get you here won't work to get you there.*

We want to help your team meet the new realities of this new postpandemic world. Against challenging odds your team stands ready to press toward the new vision God has given you to build your church, fulfill your mission, grow your organization or business, bless your community, and participate in the redemptive work that God is *still* doing. Of course, he never stopped working, despite the sometimes overwhelming challenges that are now largely in the rearview mirror.

But you're probably recognizing, like so many, that the status quo just won't cut it anymore. Though the mission hasn't changed, the ground has shifted dramatically! Leaders who will excel in this brave new world will embrace and lead from the realities previously listed, building resilient teams that will be able to face anything.

Resilient teams will enable you to lead in new directions that you haven't yet even considered. Indeed, that is one of the great promises of teams. As Harvard professor Amy Edmondson wrote, "When people put their heads together, truly intent on learning from each other, they can almost always come up with a solution that is better than anyone could come up with alone. This is teaming at its best."[7]

We want to help you build teams that enable you to solve challenging problems and face an unknown future together. That's what's ahead in this book.

THE ROADMAP TO A RESILIENT TEAM

In the organizational world, teams are ubiquitous, but "high-performance teams are extremely rare," according to Jon Katzenbach and Douglas Smith, authors of one of the leading marketplace books on effective teams.[8] You've likely served on many teams, but chances are good that you've rarely or never experienced a truly high-performance team. This book intends to change that, leading you step-by-step through a process that will result in a thriving, high-performance, resilient team. To make the most of this book, we urge you to not just *read* the book. Instead, take time to *do* the book with your team so that you will see much fruit from your time investment in this book.

But let's not get too far ahead. You may be asking, What is a high-performance, thriving, resilient team?

First, what is a team? It is not just a group of people that report to the same manager or who work in proximity to one another. Borrowing from one of the leading resources on teams, we affirm that a team is "a small number of people with complementary skills who are committed to a common purpose, set of performance goals, and approach for which they hold themselves mutually accountable."[9] Of course, there are several more definitions, but we appreciate this one because it offers six definitional criteria that any group of people must possess to form a team. Deployed appropriately, effective teams are a "means, not the end" in a quest toward higher organizational performance.[10]

Though teams that meet those six definitional criteria will generally outperform groups that do not, we're not satisfied with mediocre teams. Instead, we seek high-performance, thriving, resilient teams—teams that get stuff done, flourish in the process, and strengthen their performance capacity as they work together. Let's unpack that description.

Second, what teams are high-performing, thriving, and resilient? A *high-performance team* accomplishes both short- and long-term goals. They are potent; they get stuff done. They accomplish their ministry, organizational, or business goals in the short-term, building momentum to fulfill long-term goals as well. They make, implement, and evaluate key decisions and execute their tasks with excellence, maintaining cohesiveness along the way.[11] We want to help you ignite your team to deliver the goods in whatever space you are in and to excel in the work that you do, whatever that is. But that's not the whole story.

Members of *thriving teams* flourish in the process of working together, experiencing the satisfaction that can come only from a hard-fought victory. You will know you're on a great team "when you can't wait to get to the team meeting because it's exhilarating, fun, important and makes you feel like a grown-up."[12] Those team experiences are enjoyable and fruitful. We want to help your team flourish in your work together.

Finally, *resilient teams* grow strong by learning pivotal lessons along the journey that increase the team's capacity for leadership to face anything that comes in the future.[13] One recent study identified four critical characteristics of resilient teams: candor, resourcefulness, compassion, and humility—each of which is deployed to support one another as they accomplish their goals and grow through the process.[14] Members of resilient teams engage honestly with one another, knowing the candor they cultivate translates to strength and sustainability. Quite frankly, too many teams don't duke it out *inside* the room as they build their teams so they're prepared to duke it out *outside* the room as they tackle their projects and pursue their goals. Likewise, when you dance around issues *inside* the boardroom, you won't be able to act with boldness *outside* of it. But when you pursue radical candor as you work together as a team and learn hard-fought lessons along the way, you'll develop the strength—the resilience—to deal with anything this crazy world throws at your team. We want to help you strengthen your team so that you are prepared to handle whatever comes your way in the future.

Your church, ministry, or organization needs more high-performing, thriving, resilient teams, and we've written this book to help you on your journey toward becoming that kind of team.

The research is clear: typically it takes six months or more to develop a high-performance team. The forty targeted action steps in this book will put you on a solid, wise, seasoned path on that journey and even accelerate your progress. While you'll never be done building an unbreakable team, even after completing these forty steps, you will have launched a process across those forty steps that will continue to reap tangible benefits as you continue building your team.

HOW TO WORK THROUGH THIS BOOK

In the chapters that follow, you'll find eight movements, each with five action steps. Ideally, you would work sequentially through the movements as a team. But we know that's not practical or feasible for many of you. That's okay. You can also work through them as an individual, looking for key opportunities to infuse your learnings into your team's work.

If you can process this book as a team, and we hope you do, here's our suggested framework.

If you and your team are overachievers, you might try to tackle (or at least start) one movement each week, and one action step each weekday. But if you are like most teams, you'll need to take a four-to-six-month stretch (think quarter, semester, or season) to engage these forty action steps.

> *If you are like most teams, you'll need to take a four-to-six month stretch to engage these forty action steps.*

You might want to schedule a few full- or half-day offsites to work through a few action steps at a time. On our *The Resilience Factor* website (www.resiliencefactor.info), you'll find our ideal plan (that is, if time and money were no object and real-life constraints don't exist). Perhaps it will give you some vision to structure a plan that works for you and your team.

Don't rush, but don't lag either. Give this process the time it requires, but work with some pace, and you'll likely reap the team you've been dreaming about. Drag it out, let other things drown your focus on improving your team, and you'll find yourself right where you are today a year from now. Develop a realistic timeline to work through these eight movements, and then commit to doing the work—week in and week out. Then watch what God does with your discipline and effort. Although you can spread out your engagement with this book over as long as you need, we suggest that you follow through the chapters (movements) sequentially, not skipping ahead. The earlier movements provide foundations for those that follow.

To help facilitate and simplify your team's transformation, each movement contains several "Now It's Your Turn" exercises, some of which you'll do individually, and others you'll complete as a team. Each one seeks to help you apply and drive home the action steps laid out in this book. Take the time to do them; we've even provided room in the book for you to write directly on these pages.

If you must process the book on your own because you are not able to process it with your team, don't fret. Instead, work through it on your own. As you do, you'll be able to better name what is working and what isn't on your team, and you'll glean numerous moves you can make to try to make incremental change. As opportunities present themselves, you can ask insightful questions, infuse intentionality in your discussions and deliberations, direct discussions, and present new ways of working together. You might even find that you become a coach in disguise, aiding your team in working and relating better. As you get into the "Now It's Your Turn" activities, do all that you can on your own, and from time to time consider asking a teammate or two to go through the activity with you.

By the way, you'll see that we spend very little time making arguments for *why* you should do ministry as a team or *why* you should build a better team. We assume you're already convinced and want to know *how*. That said, if you want more of the *why*, including a biblical basis for teams and a research-based framework for thriving teams, see Ryan and Warren's previous book, *Teams That Thrive: Five Disciplines of Collaborative Church Leadership*.

THIS BOOK IS FOR TEAM LEADERS AND TEAM MEMBERS

Whether you are a designated team leader or one of several team members, this book is for you.

We'll write to the whole team throughout this book with a hopeful assumption that as a team you can determine how you can best engage to reach your goals. However, we know that some of our readers may not have leadership authority in their teams; if this is the case with you, you will need to consider how the exercises presented can be best accomplished in your context. Perhaps as a team you can make recommendations and then propose them to your team leader or another leader in your organization.

If you're a designated leader, don't forget that leadership is far more about what you do than what title you hold. So, as you read through this book, lead your team through it. Take action. Invite reflection and honest discussion. Talk about the elephant(s) in the room. Go first in ways that set an example. Make changes, even when they are hard. When you do, your team members will see clearly that you are committed to growth, and hopefully feel compelled to do the same.

Remember the role of a good team leader changes as a team develops.[15] In the early stages of a team the group needs a confident, directive leader (but not too dominant). But as the group members engage more and seek to take more ownership over the group, the effective group leader steps back a bit, inviting others to take on more leadership. Then, once the team is a high-functioning team, it's often hard to even identify the team's formal leader, as each member of the team shares various leadership responsibilities. So, if you're your team's designated leader, lead with some strength as you begin, but be ready to step back as others step forward and bid for leadership.

That's plenty of introduction—let's get to work. The world needs your resilient team.

> ***Note about the front cover:*** The design evokes the idea of resilience, where each yellow strand is under stress but none is broken. When the strands mesh and link together in a healthy way, they are unbreakable. Our desire is that God would use this book to catalyze your team's resilience, like this image.

PRAY AND ASSESS YOUR SITUATION (STEPS 1-5)

YOU CAN BUILD A RESILIENT TEAM THAT CAN FACE ANYTHING

IF YOU'RE LIKE MOST PEOPLE, you've lived through enough mediocre-at-best team experiences that you've come to accept and even expect more of the same. Perhaps without realizing it, you've lost the vision for a high-performance team to lead or contribute to a thriving organization. Maybe you also lack both the imagination of how your team could be better as well as the inspiration to even try. But renewed hope and momentum await! As you begin your journey toward building a resilient team, this chapter will help you reflect on your situation; seek God for his perspective, vision, and call; look deeply into the challenges you've faced; and set the stage for your team's transformation.

Let's fast for three days to seek the Lord."

With the news of the pandemic hitting hard in March 2020, Léonce called the leadership team of Renovation Church—the congregation he and his wife, Breanna, founded in 2011—to fast and pray on what to do next.

Like so many churches, the Renovation team decided to take all their worship gatherings online. It was a massive undertaking, requiring an incredibly quick turnaround.

A fantastic marketing group pulled off the filming and editing for that first digital service. The team gathered late on Saturday to record worship and the message live, without any rehearsal. God was kind and blessed their efforts beyond what they could have possibly accomplished in their own strength.

For over a year Renovation Church gathered only digitally in every conceivable way, including prayer, small groups, and member meetings. It took a great deal of effort and innovation to accomplish, but through several rounds of prayer and fasting, God met them every time.

A year later, when considering whether to launch physical gatherings again in a new location and without a certificate of occupancy (more on that in another book), the team—and the entire church— went back to what they knew—praying, fasting, and waiting for God's guidance and favor.

God met them there and has met them at every juncture since.

If you are going to be a part of building an unbreakable team, all the work we will set before you over these eight movements must be rooted in prayer. Certainly, "for unless the LORD builds the house, those who labor, labor in vain" (Psalm 127:1).

STEP 1: FAST, PRAY, AND SEEK GOD

Did you read the version of Nehemiah's story where he watched a few home remodeling shows on HGTV, decided that this was the year to do a fixer-upper in his hometown of Jerusalem, told his friends "I've got this," and rode off into the sunset full of great expectations?

We didn't either. Nor did we read the version where he heard the news about his beloved city still being in ruins, made a snide remark of "what else is new?" and promptly turned his attention to other more enjoyable tasks.

Against our cultural backdrop, what we read in Nehemiah's story is almost paradoxical: a skilled leader with incredible insight, intelligence, and vision, who, despite all his strengths, still took the time to place himself and his work before God.

We can imagine that when you read our bold call to fast and pray right out of the gate, especially in the context of a leadership and teams book, it probably feels a little strong. The challenge also may feel so Christian that it seems trite.

Yet, at the core of every great God-centered movement are women and men committed to that very thing. Does a season of seeking God diminish the roles of hard work, learning, grit, or vision? Absolutely not. But consider doing what is highlighted throughout biblical history and beyond. Respond to your leadership moment just as Nehemiah did: bowing before God and seeking him with all you have.

> *Respond to your leadership moment just as Nehemiah did: bowing before God and seeking him with all you have.*

The familiar story of Nehemiah 1:1–2:8 offers a powerful vision of what it looks like to prayerfully seek God's face. Take a few minutes now to meditate on how he prayed after hearing that the Jewish remnant in Jerusalem was in great distress, helpless with the city's walls broken down. Notice the bold actions he took.

NOW IT'S YOUR TURN

As you read the following verses, take the time to reflect on whether it is necessary to take a day and seek God before you do anything else on your team-transformation journey. As you seek God and what he has for you and your team in this next season, ask God to

- Reveal his desires and plans for your team.
- Show you anything you need to repent of, such as ways you haven't honored him through your team, ways you have been dependent on self and not him, and ways that you have hurt or diminished your teammates.
- Give you divine insight into what you need to see and understand to be able to build a resilient team of great impact.

As soon as I heard these words I *sat down* and *wept* and *mourned* for days, and I continued *fasting* and *praying* before the God of heaven. And I said, "O LORD God of heaven, the great and awesome God who keeps covenant and steadfast love with those who love him and keep his commandments, let your ear be attentive and your eyes open, to *hear the prayer* of your servant that *I now pray before you day and night* for the people of Israel your servants, *confessing the sins* of the people of Israel, which we have sinned against you. Even I and my father's house have sinned. We have acted very corruptly against you and have not kept the commandments, the statutes, and the rules that you commanded your servant Moses. Remember the word that you commanded your servant Moses, saying, 'If you are unfaithful, I will scatter you among the peoples, but if you return to me and keep my commandments and do them, though your outcasts are in the uttermost parts of heaven, from there I will gather them and bring them to the place that I have chosen, to make my name dwell there.' They are your servants and your people, whom you have redeemed by your great power and by your strong hand. O Lord, *let your ear be attentive to the prayer* of your servant, and to the prayer of your servants who delight to fear your name, and give success to your servant today, and grant him mercy in the sight of this man." (Nehemiah 1:4-11, emphasis added)

Don't skip this particular prayer! God has a vision and a plan for your team that will exceed your wildest dreams. Take some time to pray as Nehemiah modeled—as individuals and as a team. If you are so inclined, even take some time to fast and thus open up those deep spiritual pathways. Talk to God and invite him to speak to you. Seek his future for your team. God has plans for you, plans for your welfare, for your future, and for hope. Take this first step and open your hearts and minds to that possibility; you might be surprised how grand God's dream for you is!

STEP 2: MINE WHAT HURTS

Never-ending restrictions. Athletic seasons missed. Graduations downplayed. Sickness. Resignations. Closed doors. Fractured relationships. Crushed dreams. Isolation. Death.

The pandemic years wreaked havoc on our routines, relationships, and resolve. We experienced great disruption, loss, and strain. Have you taken the time to mine the great pain that you, your team, and your organization experienced?

In step one you took the time to fast and pray and seek God's voice and vision for your team. Carrying forward Nehemiah's story, we believe through this process you'll acknowledge pain and loss while realizing that today is not the last day in your story.

God is not done with you, nor is he finished with your ministry or organization. He has more for you, but the way to move forward is first to come face-to-face with the sovereign God and with the depths of your pain.

> *Great teams make ordinary individuals look extraordinary.*

Like it or not, great visions are often driven by great pain. Consider the civil rights movement. Though there was a myriad of factors that led to its sharp rise and very public impact, it is widely considered to have been catalyzed by the 1955 murder of Emmett Till and his mother's insistence that her son have an open-casket funeral in Chicago. The streets were quite literally lined with people, all waiting to gaze at the disfigured face of this young boy. National news outlets covered the incident, the FBI was sent to Mississippi to investigate, and soon after, at the convergence of many streams of pain and distress, the civil rights movement was born.

Though there were a few prominent voices at the head of the movement, such as Dr. Martin Luther King Jr. and John Lewis, it was truly a nationally focused team of teams' effort that brought about so many successes. If not for the work of the Southern Christian Leadership Conference and the Student Nonviolent Coordinating Committee, there would have been no civil rights movement. Great teams make ordinary individuals look extraordinary. But even a great team cannot avoid the pain often associated with great movements. Great pain launches great movements.

Great pain and challenges laid the foundation of the largest-attendance church in the United States, Life.Church, led by Craig

Groeschel. Though many people know Life.Church and Craig's popular leadership podcast, many do not know the story of Craig and his wife, Amy, and their humble beginnings. Léonce was once in a gathering where Craig vulnerably shared part of his and Amy's origin story. Craig shared the great pain they endured at the beginning of their ministry, none worse than the coup staged by his then-best friend and coplanter. The ministry already felt a bit on the ropes. Several moves, a denominational rejection of his calling, and initial meetings in the Groeschels' garage did not exactly feel like a strong start. On top of all that tumult, Craig's friend and coplanter took nearly half the congregation away over a minor theological disagreement. Craig thought the new church was done, but God had other plans. It was clear from Craig's story that he and Amy mined their pain, counted their losses, looked to God, and kept moving forward.

What if Craig and Amy had given up? What if they had failed to mine their pain so that they could then birth an incredible church? One of the great church stories of our generation may very well have gone unrealized.

Before we go any further, though, we should clarify something. We do not equate size with success. A big church or a profitable business doesn't equal success. Rather, we believe the biblical notion of success involves both faithfulness and fruitfulness. Therefore, as we discuss success and results throughout this book, we aim toward both faithfulness and fruitfulness. In this example, the Groeschels were faithful, and over many years they've also seen fruitful ministry.

NOW IT'S YOUR TURN

Once you have acknowledged that life, in varying degrees, has wreaked havoc on you and your team over the last few years, you're ready to take the next step in your journey toward a resilient team. **Exercise 1.1** will help you do this.

EXERCISE 1.1—Naming the pain and the loss you and your team have experienced

1. People and relationships lost

2. Cherished programs no longer running as successfully as in the past

3. Traditions lost that will never recover

4. Personal losses and disappointments

STEP 3: COMMIT TO RADICAL CANDOR

As a young leader, Ryan was given the profound gift of radical candor by a supervisor named Kelvin. After Ryan was previously rejected for a college student leadership role, a position opened up and Kelvin wanted to offer him the job. But first, Kelvin, after leading Ryan for a year, told Ryan he wanted to write him a letter and explain some of his concerns with Ryan stepping into that role. When Ryan got the letter, he gingerly opened it. It was nearly two single-spaced pages with small print. The first paragraph was great: "Ryan, I think you're a great leader. People follow you. You can accomplish just about whatever you want with people. You're gifted."

However, the tone shifted at the beginning of the second paragraph: "But, Ryan, I've noticed that you tend to use people to get what you want. It seems that people are more a means to you than an end. You mobilize people to help you achieve, and then you leave them while you move forward to the next task." Cue the lump in Ryan's throat. The rest of the letter provided examples of Ryan's use-and-abuse style of leadership and unpacked Kelvin's concerns. Then, in the last paragraph, he lovingly invited Ryan to chat through these concerns.

Ryan remembers that follow-up meeting vividly. It was a beautiful Colorado day. He and Kelvin sat by the lake on their college campus and talked. Kelvin made his point: there were serious things Ryan needed to work on as a leader. Ryan cried. Hard. Kelvin put his arm around him. He cared for Ryan. He loved Ryan enough to say the challenging things he needed to hear and then walk beside him while he grew as a leader. Kelvin offered Ryan the job that day, and Ryan happily accepted. Then, throughout that year, Kelvin mentored Ryan and helped him begin to become a different kind of leader.

Through that letter and the talk by the lake, Kelvin showed that he loved Ryan enough to wound him. Kelvin was a faithful friend.

Solomon says something about this too: "Faithful are the wounds of a friend; profuse are the kisses of an enemy" (Proverbs 27:6). Your team must learn to be faithful friends to one another, occasionally wounding one another out of deep love, a healthy relationship framework, and a sincere commitment to your mission.

In both the personal and organizational worlds, feedback is the breakfast of champions. Conflict (properly handled) is the fuel that drives great teams.[1] That's because the best teams deeply value feedback and ensure that feedback is frequent, candid, and flows in all directions.[2] There is zero chance that your team will become resilient if it cannot cultivate an environment of radical candor, one in which teammates care for both their mission and their teammates so much that they are willing to directly and appropriately challenge them for the good of the team and one another.

The best teams deeply value feedback.

But here's the deal: you'll never experience radical candor as a team if your team doesn't feel psychologically safe. Harvard professor Amy Edmondson suggests that psychological safety is a "shared belief held by members of a team that the team is safe for interpersonal risk taking."[3]

NOW IT'S YOUR TURN

Take a few minutes to assess your team's current sense of psychological safety (see **Exercise 1.2**[4]), and then—if you can muster it—attempt to talk about your scores.

Of course, it is no secret that it takes a while to build a culture of radical candor, but there is no better time than now to get started or improve on your current level. Take a few minutes to respond in **Exercise 1.3** with as much honesty—radical candor—as you can, identifying how radical candor has served you in the past and how it might open up important opportunities for you as a team.

As leadership guru Max De Pree famously stated, "The first responsibility of a leader is to define reality."[5] Defining reality requires both great discernment and brutal honesty. Too often leaders lack the vision to discern what's going on because they're afraid of what they might find. But resilient teams know that the way forward requires radical candor about the most uncomfortable reality.

EXERCISE 1.2—Measuring your team's psychological safety

1. If I make a mistake on this team, it won't be held against me.

DISAGREE ⟵⟶ AGREE

☐ ☐ ☐ ☐ ☐

2. On this team, it is easy to bring up difficult problems and tough issues without blowback.

DISAGREE ⟵⟶ AGREE

☐ ☐ ☐ ☐ ☐

3. It is easy to ask other members of this team for help on a project or task.

DISAGREE ⟵⟶ AGREE

☐ ☐ ☐ ☐ ☐

4. No one on this team deliberately acts to undermine my sincere efforts.

DISAGREE ⟵⟶ AGREE

☐ ☐ ☐ ☐ ☐

5. On this team, people are accepted for being different.

DISAGREE ⟵⟶ AGREE

☐ ☐ ☐ ☐ ☐

6. We encourage each other to take risks.

DISAGREE ⟵⟶ AGREE

☐ ☐ ☐ ☐ ☐

7. When I work with other members of my team, I feel that my unique skills and talents are valued and utilized.

DISAGREE ⟵⟶ AGREE

☐ ☐ ☐ ☐ ☐

TOTALS

DISAGREE ⟵⟶ AGREE

☐ ☐ ☐ ☐ ☐

EXERCISE 1.3—Identifying how radical candor affects your team

1. Reflect on a moment on a past team when radical candor opened an important door for your team to walk through.

2. Reflect on a time when a *lack* of radical candor prevented your team from needed growth or eventually sacked the team.

3. Identify one concern you'd like to raise with your team, all in the interest of developing a culture of radical candor.

4. Now make a specific list: itemize up to three challenges that are standing in the way of your team's success, and prepare to share with your team.

STEP 4: KILL THE SACRED COWS

It was a cold December morning in 2020. Nine months into the pandemic, Léonce and his senior leadership team were feeling all the pain points that countless other teams in varying fields were feeling all over the nation.

Renovation Church had not gathered physically for nine months. Predictably, there had been many meetings among his senior leadership team and even some high-emotion debates on how to move forward, when they should regather, and what the future might look like for the church if the pandemic continued with such strength and persistence.

Prominent in many of these discussions was the financial situation of the church. Though 85 percent of their financial giving was already happening online when the pandemic started, when people stopped gathering, giving was one of the first things to suffer.

After reviewing the year-end financial report, Léonce knew layoffs were inevitable. The thought weighed heavy on him and his team. After much prayer and discussion, Léonce and the Renovation team made a decision few would make: he fired his wife.

Can you imagine that conversation? Can you imagine the exchange of emotions? Can you imagine the tensions you would have to navigate?

His wife, Breanna, was his best teammate and cofounder of the church. She worked hard, serving in both worship and leading women's ministry. But, when examining *valuable* versus *vital* roles, she—as a member of the leadership team—agreed that her paid role was valuable but not vital in that season. Take heart: their marriage is still thriving, and—as tends to be the case with great teammates—though she is no longer on staff, she still faithfully serves the church.

Have you ever had to fire your spouse? Unlikely. But the underlying point of that question is one more general and applicable—are you willing to do the hard thing for the sake of the mission, vision, and health of your team and organization?

Unfortunately, for many teams the evidence says *no*. Often we are not willing to do the hard things: kill the sacred cow (note: Léonce is not likening his wonderful wife to a cow!), release the troubled teammate, or step down ourselves, even if it means greater thriving for the team and organization. But if you are going to have a resilient team, then doing hard things will have to be the norm, not the exception.

In the past few days, you have likely identified some things that you know are standing in the way of your team's success. It's time to do the hard thing that needs to be done.

Here are four ways to effectively yet tactfully kill the sacred cow— any time-honored, much-loved tradition that has lost its effectiveness:

1. *Honor your mission.* Frame change within the pursuit of your mission. (If you're not quite sure what that is, hold on until you work through movement two).

2. *Be kind, yet direct.* Explain the brutal realities you are facing and acknowledge how difficult and painful this change will be.

3. *Talk in seasons.* Explain that a program, person, or role served you and your organization well in a previous season, but that the future requires different investments and initiatives.

4. *Engage the second conversation.* Don't expect that you can have one conversation. Instead, follow up a couple of weeks down the road and meet with the persons deeply affected to hear their hearts and care for their souls amid the change.

STEP 5: DREAM THE IMPOSSIBLE

Let yourself begin to dream again. Just as the body prioritizes central organ function in extreme stress, your team likely focused its energy primarily on staying alive during the pandemic's great disruption, stress, and resetting. Not surprisingly, you've likely set aside the will or the permission to dream, to envision anew the possibilities for a greatly expanded mission. But now's the time to dream again.

As you dream, remember that far too many people think they're leading, but in reality, they're not leading—they're managing. As we previously explained, management upholds what is, while leadership involves making improvements and creating direction. If your team isn't commissioned simply to maintain the status quo, then don't!

Remember, leaders are dreamers. They imagine the world in a way that others cannot or will not. One of the greatest leaders in history is Joseph. His story is filled with twists and turns, pains and losses, surprises and disappointments, and nation-shaping accomplishments—but it began with a dream.

> Now Joseph had a dream, and when he told it to his brothers they hated him even more. He said to them, "Hear this dream that I have dreamed: Behold, we were binding sheaves in the field, and behold, my sheaf arose and stood upright. And behold, your sheaves gathered around it and bowed down to my sheaf." (Genesis 37:5-7)

As is often the case, Joseph's dream was too audacious for some of the people around him, but it did not keep him from dreaming it (though perhaps he should have been wiser in how he shared it).

Joseph's story indicates that every dream he had came true and that his leadership and ultimately the direction of the team that surrounded him was forecast by his dream. His dream not only came true, but it found favor with the Pharaoh, elevated him from a pit to the palace, and most importantly, saved the lives of multiple nations—including his brothers who betrayed him because of his dream.

There are likely a whole host of reasons—pandemic notwithstanding—that you may have ceased to dream boldly in the last season. Today, determine that a new season is on the horizon, and you will dream again. If it is a God-given dream—consistent with Scripture and spiritually discerned—then nothing and no one can keep it from coming to fruition.

NOW IT'S YOUR TURN

Before you move forward, take some time to share your dreams articulated in **Exercise 1.4** with your teammates. See if God leads you to any common dreams.

EXERCISE 1.4—Boldly dreaming into the future

1. When thinking about people to serve or reach, I imagine . . .

2. When thinking of the quality and health of our team, I imagine . . .

3. When thinking of our team's mission and purpose, I imagine . . .

4. When thinking of our organization's impact and health, I imagine . . .

5. When thinking of my personal goals, I imagine . . .

In movement two we'll help you pursue those dreams as you develop a captivating purpose that compels extraordinary commitment from each of your team members.

> *To lean into the uncomfortable, unpredictable future, you need the resilience factor.*

Today is the day to resolve to lead forward with a resilient team. To lean into the uncomfortable, unpredictable future, you need the resilience factor, and if you've already come this far, you are well on your way toward developing a powerful team that can face anything together.

END-OF-CHAPTER SUMMARY AND ACTION ITEMS

If you forget everything else, remember this as you work to take stock of your situation and the opportunity before you:

1. Engage a posture of humility before God, acknowledging your weakness and reliance on him, and listening for his vision for you and your team.

2. Name, embrace, and process the pain you've experienced—in your life, among your team, and within your church, organization, or ministry.

3. Commit to engaging one another with radical honesty driven by a true love for one another and great devotion to your mission.

4. Take bold action to eliminate the sacred cows in your midst, especially those that seem the most untouchable.

5. Dream because the last chapter of your story hasn't yet been written.

Reflection and Discussion Questions

1. What was the most useful or helpful insight you read in this movement?

2. Be frank: To what extent are you still dreaming big things for

your team and for the organization you serve? What has gotten in the way of dreaming new visions?

3. At this moment, what excites each of you most about recasting a strong vision for your team and stepping forward into what God has for you in this next season?

4. What did you do or learn this week that will be most useful to this team moving forward?

5. How do you carry forward what you learned here?

Take It Deeper

1. Talk with a trusted mentor about a sacred cow that's holding you back personally or professionally. Seek advice on what it could look like for you to boldly act on that matter.

2. Calendar a consistent time each week when you can situate yourself before God as Nehemiah did. Repent, seek God's face, and plan for and dream about what God has next for your leadership.

3. Thank a friend, coworker, or mentor who has been a faithful friend to you. Consider who God might be calling you toward so you can be a faithful friend to them.

4. Move on to the next movement, carrying with you the action steps you identified in this movement.

CLARIFY YOUR PURPOSE (STEPS 6-10)

**YOUR TEAM'S PURPOSE CAN BE
SO CLEAR THAT IT COMPELS
EXTRAORDINARY COMMITMENT**

TEAMS COHERE AROUND PURPOSE. But for too many teams, a lack of a clear and compelling purpose hides behind the problems with people, personalities, time, or trust that clamor for attention. The root of powerless teams that can't gain traction and then fall apart when the going gets tough is often a purpose problem. In this chapter we'll help you get your purpose right, such that it becomes so clear that it compels extraordinary commitment. You'll clarify what you're fighting for, discuss the boundaries that frame your team's efforts, and craft a 5C purpose (one that is clear, compelling, challenging, calling-oriented, and consistently held). When you do, you'll build a powerful foundation for your team's interaction.

This is a football." The words rolled from Hall of Fame coach Vince Lombardi's lips with ease. The thirty-eight men who stared back at him had to be curious about his angle. After all, they were members of the Green Bay Packers football team who had been just minutes from capturing the highest prize in their sport a season before. But here they were at the start of training camp in 1961 and their coach, holding a pigskin in his hand, said to them with earnestness, "gentlemen, this is a football."

Why? one might wonder. Purpose. Coach Lombardi reminded his men of the central purpose of their team, in its most elemental form. If they could remember their root purpose—to play good, fundamental football—anything was possible.

> *When a team is clear on its purpose, nothing is impossible!*

In his bestselling book *When Pride Still Mattered: A Life of Vince Lombardi*, David Maraniss explains what unfolded when Lombardi walked into training camp that summer. "He took nothing for granted. He began a tradition of starting from scratch, assuming that the players were blank slates who carried over no knowledge from the year before. . . . He began with the most elemental statement of all."[1]

Six months later, the Green Bay Packers beat the New York Giants 37–0 to win the NFL championship.

To form a winning team, you can take nothing for granted. You must be continually reminded of the core of why your team exists, your most fundamental purpose. In fact, "no team can rethink its purpose, approach, or performance goals too many times."[2] In short, when a team is clear on its purpose, nothing is impossible!

STEP 6: FOCUS ON WHAT YOU ARE FIGHTING FOR

Do you know what your team is fighting for? Maybe it's . . .

- clean water where it's never existed
- people who truly do life together
- finding every orphan a home
- marriages that make spouses holy and not just happy
- families that stick together through the madness of life
- workplaces where people love to work
- dads who love their kids well
- communities who journey through the messiness of life
- cleaner bathrooms that promote greater health
- crowded streets in heaven made of gold

What is it for you? What you're fighting for, as leadership author David Burkus suggests, might be a problem you're trying to solve, an injustice you're trying to resolve, something you're trying to prove, or a slice of a better world you are trying to create.[3]

It's time to resurface your big *why*. Most organizations and many teams start with a noble purpose, but over time the daily rhythms of doing the work tend to crowd out the powerful purpose that once fueled and inspired the pioneers and the builders. Before long, they forget the big *why* they're fighting for.

Perhaps you've forgotten too. Or lost clarity of focus. Not anymore. Your dreams used to live in the recesses of your mind too, but you have begun to dream again. Now you're ready to fight for it.

Teams that know what they are fighting for—and then actually fight for it—far outpace other teams that are fuzzy on their mission. A common purpose "cultivates a strong shared bond that connects participants to each other in pursuit of their purpose" and then propels them forward to accomplish that powerful purpose.[4] The benefits extend beyond small teams too. Entire companies that start with and lean into their *why* tend to dramatically outperform those that focus more on *what* they do than *why* they do it.[5]

NOW IT'S YOUR TURN

It's time to reclaim your big *why*, the thing your team is fighting for. But that's not always easy, because the thing you are fighting for is often buried under layers of organizational jargon and habits. It might take some digging to get to it. **Exercise 2.1** is a tool to aid you in your big dig.

In this exercise, you start with the descriptive statement of what you are doing (leading a team), and then ask, "Why is that important?" five times. After a few whys, you'll get down to the fundamental reasons your team, and in most cases, your organization exists. And when you do, you'll be ready to articulate more of why you and your organization needs a resilient team. [6] If you need inspiration, watch Simon Sinek's TED Talk, "How Great Leaders Inspire Action."[7]

EXERCISE 2.1—Digging in to your five whys

1. What does your team do?

2. Why?

3. Why? (What's the why behind the "why"?)

4. Why? (What's the why behind that "why"?)

5. Why? (Can you voice a why behind that?)

6. So, what are you fighting for? (If possible, voice it in twenty words or less.)

STEP 7: ACKNOWLEDGE AND DEFINE
YOUR TEAM'S BOUNDARIES

Every team's work is bounded by contextual and organizational factors. You're hemmed in by your broader organization's vision, mission, strategy, and values—and that's a good thing. Just as "good fences make good neighbors,"[8] teams that respect their boundaries find an appropriate playing field, a fertile ground where the team can discern its unique purpose.

NOW IT'S YOUR TURN

You might need to do some in-house research, but get the data you need and write down what you find—the boundaries that frame your team's work. Once you work out your team's "vision frame," diagnose the activity and purposes of every aspect of your organization accordingly.[9] Do they fall within the good boundaries of the vision frame (see fig. 2.1)?

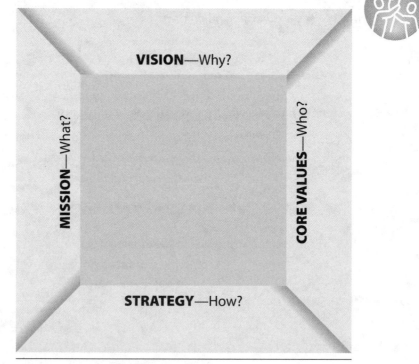

VISION—Why?

MISSION—What?

CORE VALUES—Who?

STRATEGY—How?

Figure 2.1. Capture your team vision frame

A couple of examples follow of what this can look like.

The Renovation Kids Ministry. The purpose of the Renovation Kids Ministry is to see children grow in the knowledge and love of God. This mission fits in line with and within the boundaries of the organizational vision, mission, core values, and strategy of Renovation Church.

Renovation's *vision* is to see the world awakened to the wonder of God and his transcultural church. The *mission* is to make, multiply, and deploy disciples. The *core values* are to be a Jesus-centered, socially conscious, Spirit-led, and transcultural community. And the *strategy* is to help people know God, find freedom, discover purpose, and then make a difference in the world (see fig. 2.2).

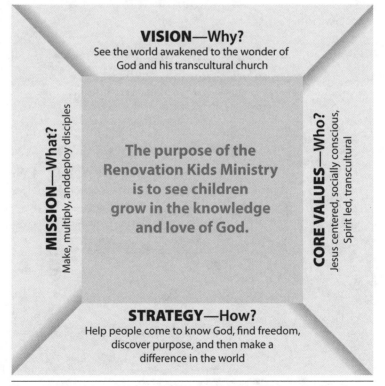

VISION—Why?
See the world awakened to the wonder of God and his transcultural church

MISSION—What?
Make, multiply, anddeploy disciples

The purpose of the Renovation Kids Ministry is to see children grow in the knowledge and love of God.

CORE VALUES—Who?
Jesus centered, socially conscious, Spirit led, transcultural

STRATEGY—How?
Help people come to know God, find freedom, discover purpose, and then make a difference in the world

Figure 2.2. The vision, mission, core values, and strategy of Renovation Church

You can see how having the purpose to see children grow in the knowledge and love of God ideally fits within the bounds of Renovation's organizational vision frame.

Department of Church and Ministry Leadership, Lancaster Bible College | Capital Seminary. The purpose of the church and ministry leadership department at LBC is to cultivate disciples and craft leaders for an interconnected world. This purpose flows directly through LBC's vision framework, which defines the institution's larger mission, values, strategies, and measures of success. Notice how LBC's mission statement frames the department's purpose: "We educate Christian students to think and live a biblical worldview (cultivate disciples) and to proclaim Christ by serving him (craft leaders) in the Church and in society (an interconnected world)." In figure 2.3 you can see that the church and ministry leadership department's specific purpose articulates their unique contribution to the greater mission of the institution.[10]

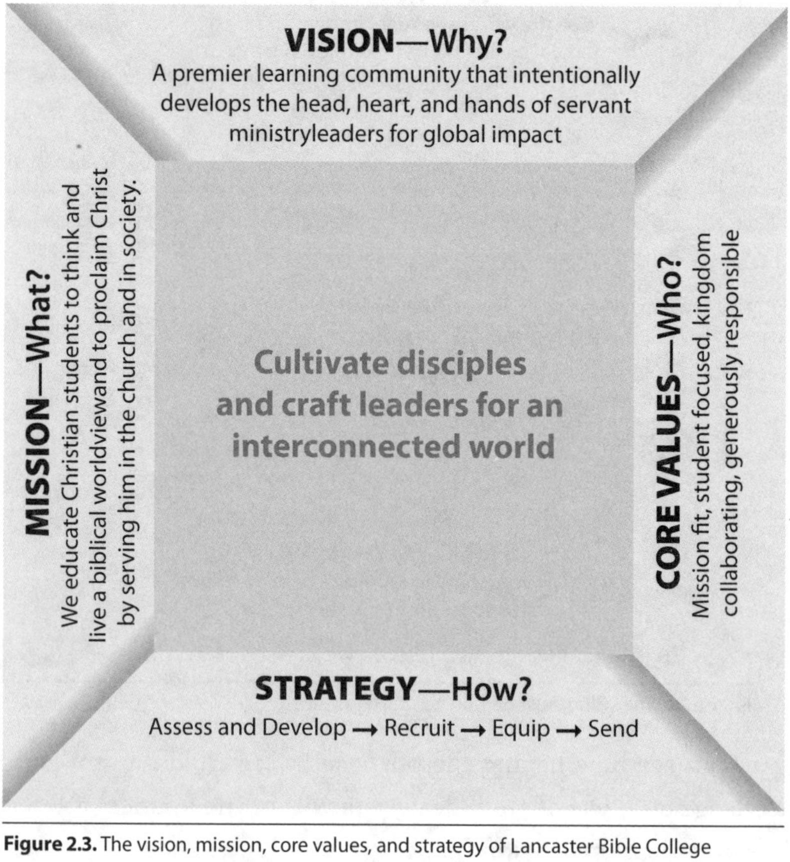

VISION—Why?
A premier learning community that intentionally develops the head, heart, and hands of servant ministryleaders for global impact

MISSION—What?
We educate Christian students to think and live a biblical worldviewand to proclaim Christ by serving him in the church and in society.

CORE VALUES—Who?
Mission fit, student focused, kingdom collaborating, generously responsible

Cultivate disciples and craft leaders for an interconnected world

STRATEGY—How?
Assess and Develop → Recruit → Equip → Send

Figure 2.3. The vision, mission, core values, and strategy of Lancaster Bible College

As you do the following exercise, you'll begin to think about how your team fits into your church or organization's wider strategy and approach. For now, just fill in the four sides of your boundary frame. Then, as you go to the next steps, you'll soon fill in that large blank part in the center.

EXERCISE 2.2—Fill in your boundary frame

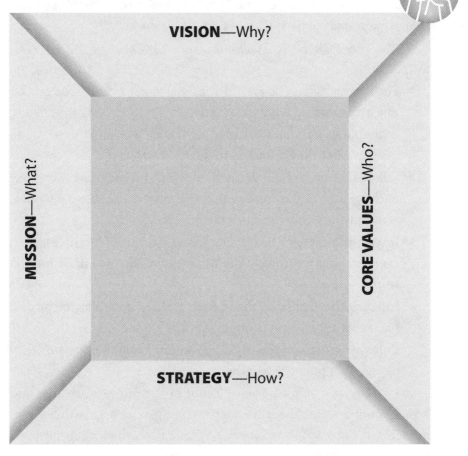

VISION—Why?

MISSION—What?

CORE VALUES—Who?

STRATEGY—How?

STEP 8: ASSESS YOUR TEAM'S SENSE OF PURPOSE

In Ryan and Warren's previous book, *Teams That Thrive: Five Disciplines of Collaborative Church Leadership*, they presented a framework to judge the quality of a team's purpose, which they called a 5C purpose.[11]

- ▣ *Clear.* Does the team's purpose paint a *clear* picture of value?
- ▣ *Compelling.* Do team members view the purpose as consequential? Does it address something that *truly matters, drawing people into it*?
- ▣ *Challenging.* To accomplish the purpose, is each member of the team required to contribute in a *meaningful and interdependent way*?
- ▣ *Calling-oriented.* Does accomplishing the purpose help members *accomplish God's calling on their lives and pursue their goals*?
- ▣ *Consistently held.* Do the members of a group *truly know the group's purpose and pursue it with fervor*?

A 5C purpose is superfuel for your team. That's because a 5C purpose will

- ▣ Focus your team's scope, so that you don't try to take on too much and end up doing very little.
- ▣ Leave plenty of good work to other teams, who don't need you to take on what they're tasked to do.
- ▣ Compel people to contribute their best to the team in the context of the group, as they realize that the most consequential work is accomplished only through collaboration.
- ▣ Inspire and energize the team, serving as a sort of invisible leader, even making a strong individual leader less essential for the team's success.
- ▣ Increase the likelihood that people will see and refer to you as a team that together gets important work done.
- ▣ Cultivate trust and relationships among team members as they pursue that purpose together.

The pursuit of a 5C purpose will result in a strong performance and a well-bonded team. That's because a team gels as it gets to work in pursuing its purpose. To accomplish a particularly challenging purpose, team members quickly realize they must trust one another and build stronger relationships with each other. As they work together to successfully navigate healthy conflict, make decisions, and produce quality work, they do so in the pursuit of purpose.[12] Trust is built in the trenches as each team pursues its unique team purpose.

But too many teams don't possess a clear sense of their team's purpose—or they wrongly assume that their purpose is clear.

When Warren and Ryan were researching *Teams That Thrive*, they asked multiple members from the same church teams to write the purpose of their respective teams. This led to a phone call. "Ryan, did we mess up on our survey?" Warren asked Ryan. "Did you read what people wrote for their team's purpose statement?"

One person wrote that the purpose of his team is to "Know Christ and make him known," while another person *on that same team* wrote her team's purpose as "To give leadership to the tasks the pastor assigned us." Warren noted that in several other churches, the disconnect between what members of the same team said was likewise night and day.

"Actually," Ryan replied, "that's truly what they said. It's really hard to believe that some of these team members were ever in the same room."

Little wonder that some teams go everywhere and nowhere. And with little passion at that!

NOW IT'S YOUR TURN

In light of these stories, take some time for each member of your team to write what they believe is your team's purpose, and then compare your responses and discuss the similarities and differences (see **Exercise 2.3**).

EXERCISE 2.3—Rating your team purpose against the 5Cs

1. In your team meeting this week, hand out a 3 x 5 card to each member and ask each one to write your team's purpose on it. Then ask everyone to rate the team purpose—from 1 to 5 (5 being the highest)—against each of the 5Cs.
2. Share what each person wrote as the purpose statement and their ratings on the 5Cs. You'll quickly learn where your team's sense of purpose is both strongest and weakest.
3. What did you learn through the exercise?

STEP 9: CRAFT YOUR TEAM'S 5C PURPOSE

Go back to that boundary frame you developed in step 7. With that context in mind, it's time to establish your team's 5C purpose by working through the following steps.

- Brainstorm the crucial tasks that your team must accomplish. List them on a whiteboard.

- Draw several large, equal-size circles spread out over a large, clear section of the board (make each one as big as possible but not touching each other so you can later write inside them). You'll need one circle for each member of your team, plus one more for your team as a collective.

- As a group, determine how each of those crucial tasks is best handled—by the team or by an individual—and then write the task in the corresponding circle that indicates who owns the task. Those tasks that go to the team should be those that require or greatly benefit from multiple perspectives, interdependence and collaborative activity, and form the foundation for your team's unique purpose. As you do this, you'll identify what your team, and your team only, can accomplish as it works together.

- Together narrow and establish your team's purpose, in line with your boundary frame, and write it down. Note: it must be different from the organization's overall purpose, as we'll explain in the next step.

- Finally, check to ensure the purpose is clear, compelling, challenging, calling-oriented, and consistently held. If it is, good. If not, continue to hone it until everyone agrees that it meets the 5C standards.

Work through these steps. Resist the urge to steal some other team's purpose. There's no one-size-fits-all approach, and the process here is as important as the product. Not only should every member of your team say "this is a winning team purpose," but they'll also feel the team growing more of a sense of *us* and the strength bonds that characterize a resilient, high-performance team. You're well on your way to a resilient team that can face anything.

NOW IT'S YOUR TURN

Use **Exercise 2.4** to write your 5C purpose.

••

EXERCISE 2.4—Developing a 5C purpose

Write your team's new 5C purpose here:

STEP 10: DRAFT THE FIRST PART OF YOUR TEAM'S CHARTER

Most likely, every staff or key volunteer in your organization has a job description. Whether it drives their work and provides an accountability structure is another matter for another discussion. In theory, at least, a good job description provides focus, clarifies expectations, delineates qualifications for job candidates, and outlines the criteria for performance evaluation.

But what about teams? What if every team in every organization had a job description? It would look like a charter that explained the team's purpose and how that purpose would be different from other teams and individuals on the team and throughout the organization.

Throughout the next several weeks you are going to build your team's charter. Your 5C purpose is the first building block; indeed, it is the foundation for your resilient team.

When it's complete, your team charter will outline your team's focus, responsibilities, duties, and qualifications for membership. It will articulate your working norms, key roles members play, an accountability structure, and the metrics you use to measure your success and continual growth. Most importantly, it will help your team avoid getting unnecessarily captured by stuff that's screaming at you (the urgent) or bogged down hashing through minutia (the unimportant) while failing to create time to talk about what's most essential for their success as a team (the truly important). Your charter will give you permission to focus on what you're fighting for and ignore the chatter that will mercilessly fight for your attention.

NOW IT'S YOUR TURN

Download the team charter template at www.resiliencefactor.info, fill out the purpose section, and then sign it.

. . . .

The world needs your team.

Do you believe that?

We need you to fight because you know (and we know) that you have something worth fighting for. Armed with a new 5C purpose, you're now ready to build an all-star cast. Movement three will help ensure your team is composed of the right team members.

END-OF-CHAPTER SUMMARY AND ACTION ITEMS

If you forget everything else, remember this as you clarify your team's purpose:

1. Unearth the big why—the thing you are fighting for—that motivates and drives your team forward.

2. Acknowledge the organizational vision, mission, goals, strategy, and values that frame your team's work so that you can color within the lines.

3. Understand the monumental value of a strong team purpose, and humbly appraise the quality of your existing team purpose.

4. Work through a collaborative process to develop your team's 5C purpose, recognizing that the process of developing your purpose is just as valuable as whatever you produce.

5. Document your team's purpose so you can regularly refer back to it, and allow it to guide your team's structure and prioritize and focus your team's efforts.

Reflection and Discussion Questions

1. What was the most useful or helpful insight you read in this movement?

2. What are the purpose problems your team is experiencing?

3. What is your team fighting for? To what extent does your team stay focused on that fight rather than others that clamor for attention?

4. How could sharpening your team's purpose enable you to move forward in growing into a resilient team?

5. What did you do or learn this week that will be most useful to this team moving forward?

Take It Deeper

1. Do an honest self-assessment: How well do you know and believe in what your team is fighting for?

2. Take the time to reflect on your organization's vision, mission, values, and strategy. Write them down somewhere that will be visible to you often.

3. Consider each of your teammates individually. Do you trust them? If the answer is yes, write the reason each one has gained your trust. If the answer is no, identify why you do not trust them and consider what you might do to work toward establishing greater trust.

4. Move on to the next steps, carrying with you the action commitments you identified in this movement.

GATHER AN ALL-STAR CAST (STEPS 11-15)

YOU DON'T HAVE TO SETTLE—
YOU CAN BUILD A TEAM OF TOP
PERFORMERS

YOU'D THINK MOST TEAMS would be made up of the people who could best contribute to the team. The sad reality for most teams is otherwise. In this chapter we'll acknowledge why people often settle for the constraints that too commonly drive team membership, but we'll also offer practical frameworks to imagine an all-star cast, how to recruit those people, and how to tactfully change team membership when necessary and allowable.

Ryan, you won't believe this," the email from an executive pastor in Southern California began. "Remember your recent workshop when I told you that I was tired of not having the right people on our leadership team but wasn't sure how to move a couple of people off the team to make room for others to join? Well, I took your advice, and we worked to clarify our purpose. A couple of weeks later, both of the people who I felt needed to move to another ministry volunteered to step back from the team! They said they aren't a good match for where the team is going. We now feel like we have the right people on our team, with room to add maybe one or two more, and we're ready to move forward."

We suspect that you can identify with parts of this pastor's story. If only all challenges could be solved in two weeks! But right now you know something's got to shift. You're just not sure how to make changes without destroying your team. Are you stuck with a team you inherited that doesn't give you the firepower you and your organization need to achieve remarkable results? Unsure how to imagine and then make the changes that need to take place? Hesitant to upset the apple cart of your current team?

Or maybe you've been humming along, not thinking about who's filling the chairs (or Zoom squares) and whether they're the right people and the right mix?

Either way, you're not alone. Once you've clarified your team's purpose as movement two outlined, it's time to make sure you've got the right people around the table and that they're optimized to make their greatest contribution.

Settle no more. Instead, build a team of top performers.

STEP 11: EVALUATE THE TEAM YOU'VE GOT

Start with an inventory. At different seasons every team needs to take a self-assessment. In many respects taking stock of a team is like taking a sabbath. It's a time to pause the work, reflect on what's been done, look up to see what God is saying, and look forward to what he has before us. Sometimes teams self-assess by every team member taking the StrengthsFinder, MBTI, or SDI and discussing their results together.[1] Other times this is done at the beginning of a new season or new fiscal year. But too often teams don't pause to take stock simply because they are so busy doing the work that they forget to reflect on the work, how it's getting done, and who is doing it. If you've ever tried to cut firewood with a dull chainsaw, you know the importance of pausing to sharpen your saw!

NOW IT'S YOUR TURN

On your own, no matter your role on the team, take a few minutes to complete **Exercise 3.1** to take stock of your team's membership.

Once you and the other members of your team have prayerfully, thoughtfully, and separately considered the strengths and contributions of each member, gather as a team and complete **Exercise 3.2**.

EXERCISE 3.1—Assessing your team members' greatest contributions

1. Write your team's purpose from movement two (you must keep this constantly front and center in any team analysis).

2. Explore the unique contributions of each member of your team.

Team member name	In what ways does this person most powerfully contribute to your team?	What are this person's key strengths in relation to your team's tasks?	What are this person's key strengths in relation to your team's cohesion and connectedness?	If this person were suddenly no longer on your team, what would your team miss most?

EXERCISE 3.2—Optimizing your team's strengths

1. Go around the room and tell each person what the other team members see that person most powerfully brings to the team.

2. Discuss the following questions:

   In an ideal situation, what additional skill, perspective, or approach would your team include that it currently does not have?

   How could you as a team get more of that skill, perspective, or approach? Consider how you could add additional team members or by up-skilling your current team members.

3. Your discussion notes:

These exercises will act like a rototiller, churning up good questions and reflections about your team's composition. Once that happens, you're ready to move to the next step.

In healthy teams, leaders model going the extra mile—even daily—to give compliments to and affirm team members. Warren is on a team like that at the Evangelical Council for Financial Accountability (ECFA). One memorable meeting ended with each person affirming the strength and contribution of each other team member. Warren remembers what hard work it was to craft a gushy but genuine sentence about each person there. It made him listen carefully to the compliments that others read about his peers on the team.

The outcome surprised him. He walked away with tons of fresh insight about the strengths each person represented and ways he and other team members could do a better job tapping into them as a team.

STEP 12: INVEST IN YOUR CURRENT TEAM MEMBERS

Now that you have taken stock of your team, it is time to identify ways you can invest in your current team members. In today's and tomorrow's leadership context the "most successful leaders . . . will be those who have the ability to develop the talents of others."[2] Take some time today to look over these ideas and decide on one or two ways you will each become better trained in a skill or perspective that will help your team. You're not finished until you have decided who will do what by when.

For example, "Within the next 48 hours, Janice will find a 15–30 minute highly practical video on the subject of conflict management and send us the link so we can all watch it before our next meeting."

Here are some options:

1. Pursue additional group training in how to be a team.

   - Bring in an expert.

   - Watch a training video together.

   - Interview an author who wrote a book about teams (hmm!).

2. Enhance technical skill in a specific area.

- Watch an online course.

- Read a book.

- Attend a conference.

- Shadow someone.

- Visit another similar organization.

- Work toward certification.

3. Better develop your strengths.

- Work with a coach.

- Take an assessment.

- Find a mentor.

The key is to identify opportunities, encourage (and grant permission to) people to engage, create space in people's schedules to do so, and hold each other accountable for follow-up. Along the way, everyone encourages each other that "we can get better as a team!"

For instance, ECFA offers several free tools to help governing boards be more effective. One is an annual board member renewal document designed to help board members evaluate whether they're able to meet the expectations or requirements of serving on the board.[3] In essence it provides a safe, face-saving way for people to decide to opt not to join a team or for the team leader to initiate a discussion on the topic. The strategy can apply to any type of team.

> *Identify opportunities, encourage engagement, create space to do so, and follow up.*

STEP 13: EMBRACE AND ENGAGE THE NECESSARY, HARD CONVERSATIONS

Sometimes it's not just about who you will add but about who you must subtract. Most people know that it would probably be good to press into hard conversations about calling, match, passion, or commitment levels, but they often struggle to develop the gumption to take action. So, first, let us help you build a sense of urgency and then equip you to handle these conversations as well as possible.

The following are reasons to engage in hard conversations.

1. You want to model biblical mandates of speaking the truth in love (Ephesians 4:15), forgiving (Matthew 6:14-15), not nursing a grudge (Leviticus 19:18; Mark 11:25), not harboring anger (James 1:20), not letting the sun go down on your anger (Ephesians 4:26), and living at peace with others whenever possible (Romans 12:18). In short, when you need to confront, a Christian's call is to keep short accounts.

2. Your organization's mission is too important to allow a significant team weakness to continue.

3. The right people will leave when the wrong people are allowed to stay.

4. You want to signal to the rest of your team that your work is consequential, and your team will be accountable for results, as you pursue both faithfulness and fruitfulness.

5. You can't afford to allow the person who is a bad fit to set the culture for everyone else. That's in essence letting the person who is a bad fit shape the group's norms and expectations.

6. You want all other members to feel safe and protected from bad behavior, such as low commitment, poor performance, mismatched talents, or other unhealthy habits.

Once you've developed the conviction and courage to have the hard conversation (and perhaps recruited a prayer partner or two), here are some tips to do it well.

1. If the issue is performance-related and can be improved, invite the person into a development plan. Outline the expectations for improvement, what you'll offer in terms of support and coaching, and a time frame to reassess how things are going. Then stick to it.

2. If the issue is simply related to a mismatch of skill and contribution to your team's purpose, then move forward.

- Acknowledge the team member's strengths and where they can make the most impact.

- Discuss your desire to see each person contribute in a place where they can make the most impact (which will be good for them and the ministry).

- Identify a plan to find a new, adjusted role. Establish a time frame to revisit your progress in moving that person to a better fit.

- Couch the entire conversation with a kingdom mindset, your fidelity to your organization or ministry's important mission, as well as your deep care and concern for the person.

3. Follow up after the hard conversation, both with the team member you've confronted and the remainder of the team. Changes within your team's membership will stir stress and challenge among others, so you must be present to the emotions and challenges that arise in the process and handle them well, realizing the hurt and distrust generated by transitions motivated by power plays and/or generated by insufficient reasons.

At this step, consider the hard but necessary conversations you need to have and begin to plan now what they are, how you'll handle them, and when you'll engage them.

STEP 14: ARTICULATE TEAM MEMBERSHIP QUALIFICATIONS AND REQUIREMENTS

Remember the team charter you began to develop on step 10? Pull it back out. Now is the time to add another section to it: "Qualifications and Requirements for Team Members."

NOW IT'S YOUR TURN

Working through these qualifications—just as you would for an individual's job description—will help you identify the unique skills and perspectives you need on your team, as well as the shared interactional behaviors you expect for your team (see **Exercise 3.3**).

••

EXERCISE 3.3—Developing qualifications and requirements for team members

1. Essential skills we need on our team:

2. Essential perspectives that must be considered by our team:

3. When we look to replace or add new team members, we will look for people who . . .

• Possess this kind of character:

• Will jibe with our team because:

• Commit to connecting with others by:

When you do this, you'll press back against the all-too-common practice of determining your team's membership by drawing a circle around a certain part of the organizational chart or by simply making a convenient choice, such as grabbing everyone whose office is nearby or who frequents the same coffee stop. Instead, you will have identified the particular mix of skills, strengths, and perspectives your team needs to be most successful, and how you will need to interact to leverage the strengths each person brings. Now, when you have to decide who should serve on your team and who shouldn't, you have a guideline to help you.

When Bill Walsh came to San Francisco to take the reins as the head coach of the 49ers, the team was in shambles. The team had a losing record, and they were consistently pummeled by their rival, the Dallas Cowboys. Enter the late Bill Walsh, now a Hall of Fame coach and considered to be the architect of the 49ers dynasty.

Coach Walsh popularized and perfected the now-renowned "West Coast offense," which paved the way for five Super Bowl victories for the 49ers. His innovations provided a frequently copied blueprint for coaches at every level of the game and propelled players such as Joe Montana, Steve Young, and Jerry Rice toward Hall of Fame careers of their own.

Walsh knew what he needed to take his team to the next level, he was versed in the mix of skills and characteristics required for them to become champions, and he was revered for bringing the best out of his players.

Walsh is credited as one of the most important figures in football in the 1980s, not just for winning but also for his intentionality in assembling a winning team. You can do the same, even if it takes time and incremental development of your existing team members.

STEP 15: LOOK BEYOND THE USUAL SUSPECTS TO ADD TO OR COMPLEMENT YOUR TEAM

At this point you've taken stock of who you have on your team and what's missing, identified the unique strengths each team member brings, put forward a plan to invest in growth, begun to consider who may not be a good fit on the team, and developed a list of key qualifications and requirements for your team members. After all of this you may realize that you need more or different people with particular skill sets, experiences, or perspectives.

When it comes to supplementing your team, you have two primary options. One is to recruit and permanently add new members to your team. The other is to ask people to join your team temporarily at strategic, intermittent times and bring their expertise.

As you ponder, consider what your optimal team size should be, assuming you're not required to have a certain number of members. You want a minimum of three and ideally five, with the logic that one personality won't unduly shape the group, but you also have the diversity of perspective, experience, and skill to benefit from collaboration.[4] At the same time, when a team goes beyond a dozen or so, then too many people remain unengaged or underutilized.

In her outstanding book, *Creating Effective Teams*, researcher Susan Wheelan explained, "successful teams contain the smallest number of members necessary to accomplish goals and tasks," with that number often landing between three and six members.[5]

Start with option 1: if you can add more team members without making the team too big, by all means do so. You have nothing to lose by shooting high! In such a case clearly describe what you are looking for and how that new person will add to and complement the team, pray, and then find them.

Either way, dream big and pray big. Reach high (the worst that can happen is that someone prays about your *ask* and says no). Also think outside the box beyond the predictable suspects. For instance, instead of just targeting grandmas, moms, and soon-to-be moms to serve in children's ministry, why not consider recruiting men? Or suppose you're on a sermon feedback team. If, for instance, you're in a church with complementarian convictions, don't just invite the preachers, all of whom would be male, to form the team that listens to and provides feedback on the sermon before it is preached. If more than half of the listeners to that sermon will be women, wouldn't you want some of them to advise on whether the illustrations connect and points convict? Maybe you'd also want to invite a college student or high schooler onto the team.

Or if you're on a team that's doing outreach into your community, would it be appropriate to tap into a community person in some way? Or maybe you are part of a team that does a lot of its work online. Do any of your members have an older relative in a retirement home who could mobilize any seniors there to join and assist you? In short, be creative and consider how you can reach higher to find the help you need to get the right staff on your team.

The reality for many readers, however, is that your team is made up of paid staff, and you don't have another paid staff spot, so you must be creative to get more firepower into your team without significant financial resources to throw at it. That's okay. The following are a few creative ways to do this.

1. Identify other people in your broader organization who have particular skills or perspectives you need, and ask them to invest a small number of hours with your team or on specific projects. Of course, this will require approval from those persons' supervisors, but you've done enough analysis about your team's needs over the last fourteen steps that you should be able to build a pretty compelling case.

2. Invite a freelancer to join you for a slice of a project. Even a small, volunteer-led ministry or church can usually find enough money to offer an outside person. "Could we pay you $200 (or whatever fits your budget) to come to our next meeting, prepared to walk us through such-and-such where none of us has expertise?"

3. Invite a volunteer leader or two with significant capacity to assist your effort. When one church in California wanted to develop a serious leadership development program, the lead pastor invited a group of three laypeople who worked in leadership education and consulting to develop the curriculum. Not only did it yield a

more robust and effective program than what the staff could have developed on their own, but it also gave those church members a meaningful way to contribute their talents to their local church, deepening their engagement and connection to the church. Remember, as you ask for help from volunteers, they might need more lead time than a paid staff member will need.

4. Don't let geography constrain you. The pandemic created many more opportunities to tap into talent that isn't local. Expertise, skill, and perspective reside everywhere, and remote work connections make it much easier to tap into them.

NOW IT'S YOUR TURN

Exercise 3.4 will help you creatively discover where to find what your team needs.

· ·

EXERCISE 3.4—Discovering where you can find what your team needs

My team needs	Where in my sphere of influence does this skill reside?

NOW IT'S YOUR TURN

As you consider inviting or bringing someone new onto your team, ask the eleven questions in **Exercise 3.5**, which will help you better understand that person and how they will fit on your team. The first four questions include suggested tools you can use to aid in discovering the unique ways a potential team member is gifted, wired, and wounded. The next seven are sometimes referred to as the seven Cs of leadership and team dynamic fit. Leverage these questions and tools to minimize the possibility of making a blind hire. Instead make an informed, thoughtful choice.

••

EXERCISE 3.5—Eleven questions to ask when bringing someone new onto your team

Question to ask	Tool or Characteristic
1. What is your spiritual vocation?	A.P.E.S.T. (apostle, prophet, evangelist, shepherd, teacher)
2. What are your spiritual gifts?	Spiritual gifts assessment
3. What is your Myers-Briggs type?	Myers-Briggs test
4. What is your Enneagram number?	Enneagram test
5. Who are you at your core?	Character
6. What drives you?	Conviction
7. How do you engage, own, and finish?	Conduct
8. Are you a fit?	Chemistry
9. What is your calling?	Clarity
10. How big is your plate?	Capacity
11. What skills do you have?	Competency

At this point, you've sought God and started to dream again, and you've addressed your team's mission and membership. Now it's time to get to work and take steps to build your team strong, effective, and resilient. The next movement will help you do just that.

END-OF-CHAPTER SUMMARY AND ACTION ITEMS

If you forget everything else, remember this as you assess and assemble your all-star cast:

1. Take time to pause and reflect on the work you are doing and whether you have the right people to best achieve your team's purpose.

2. Build into your existing team by encouraging, giving permission, and scheduling space for your team members to develop both individually and as a team.

3. Leverage hard conversations to ensure that the right people stay and the wrong people leave, rather than the other way around.

4. Articulate the unique skills and perspectives you need on your team, as well as the shared interactional behaviors you expect from your team.

5. Creatively and intentionally complement your existing team to infuse new perspectives and possibilities into the team.

Reflection and Discussion Questions

1. What was the most useful or helpful insight you read in the five steps of this movement?

2. Think of a time when you have been on a team where someone has outstayed their welcome, causing the team to settle instead of excel. If you could go back to that time now as the leader of that team, what would you do differently and why?

3. What did it feel like for each of you to think through and discuss your unique contributions to the team? How did it encourage you, and did it nudge you forward in any way?

4. What did you do or learn this week that you believe will be most useful to this team moving forward?

5. How do you carry forward what you learned here?

Take It Deeper

1. Ask one or more trusted mentors about a time when they engaged in a hard conversation like the ones discussed in step 13. Probe that situation to discover insights that might be helpful to your current situation.

2. Go the extra mile to personally tell a teammate or two how grateful you are for them and the roles they play on your team.

3. Make a list of several people who possess insights or expertise that could benefit your team. Consider people from both inside and outside your organization.

4. As you move on to the next steps, carry with you the action steps you identified this week.

GET TO WORK (STEPS 16-20)

YOU CAN MAXIMIZE THE IMPACT OF YOUR LIMITED TEAM-BUILDING TIME

EVERY LEADERSHIP BOOK TELLS YOU to build your team. But how? That's where the bad advice begins. Many focus on downright awkward team-building exercises. The problem? They may be fun, but too many simply don't work to build team trust. Sadly, with so much team-building advice available, team leaders often spin their wheels trying the latest fads on how to build their teams, when the body of research on this is clear: teams make their best progress toward gelling when they work together on a collective goal. In this chapter we'll try to inspire both team leaders and members toward a propensity to meaningful action rather than a misguided focus early in a team's life cycle on learning to get along.

The entire world—including one billion live viewers—rejoiced on the day when an entire work force of thirty-three miners emerged alive, sixty-nine days after a Chilean mine collapse had sealed them in a mountain a half-mile underground. That 2010 experience was a vivid example of a team of teams that all got to work, showing the resilience necessary to overcome incredible odds.

Teams ranged from nearly every Chilean government ministry, the US NASA space agency, and a dozen corporations from around the world. Three separate drilling teams each experimented with a different method, all working simultaneously, and yet cooperating through shared information as they learned from each other. It took approximately thirty different probes, each cutting through rock harder than granite, before the miners were found—still alive.

The drilling team that was the first to reach the miners had followed the strategy proposed by a twenty-four-year-old field engineer, Igor Proestakis. He believed that an American company's cluster hammer technology could cut through the hard rock quicker than other drills could. The operation's leader listened to him, felt that he might be right, and put his idea to work. "Despite my experience and age, he listened to me, asked questions, and gave me a chance," Proestakis said.[1]

Even the miners themselves used the team concept, resiliently grouping themselves into various survival teams. According to miner Mario Sepúlveda, "We knew that if society broke down, we would all be doomed. Each day a different person took a bad turn. Every time that happened, we worked as a team to try to keep the morale up."[2]

Oddly enough, this team didn't gather around a campfire engaging "two truths and a lie," invest a half-day to go through a nearby ropes course, or take turns doing a trust fall or weeping willow exercise before they figured out how to drill down to those trapped miners. Instead, they got to work and let their team grow together as they worked together. Your team needs to do the same.

STEP 16: FOCUS ON BUILDING TRUST IN THE TRENCHES

You've established a 5C purpose and you've taken steps to solidify your team membership in the last two movements. Now it's time to build your team by gelling it so you can become more effective and healthy.

How do you do that?

Get to work. Yes, that's right. That's the first thing you must do. As we'll explain, research indicates that the best teams start by getting to work.

Sadly, too many team leaders have been taught to build their teams on trust, as though trust is the foundation. That seems intuitive. Many think, *If our team can't trust one another, we'll fail to achieve unity, along with the corresponding results that come from a tightly bonded team.*[3]

However, while trust is necessary for high levels of performance, focusing on building trust doesn't build trust. Unfortunately, activities like the classic trust fall or sharing times where team members candidly voice their most embarrassing moments, special childhood memories, or greatest fears simply don't get the job done.

Instead, trust builds as a *byproduct* of a team's focus and pursuit of a common purpose. Certainly, it's easy to confuse the chicken and the egg here in terms of which causes the other. When people see two properties—in this case trust and performance—operating together, it's natural to seek to understand how they relate to each other. Often, though, we confuse the relationship, mistakenly thinking that trust *caused* performance. But an extensive body of literature indicates something else: when team members focus on accomplishing their purpose, they will begin to experience productive teamwork and trusting relationships.[4] In other words, first comes the work, and then comes trust. Then, as that trust builds, it engenders greater performance, which creates even more trust.

NOW IT'S YOUR TURN

If you want to build trust in your team, get to work together, using **Exercise 4.1**.

....

EXERCISE 4.1—Team-building questions to ask team members

In your next team meeting, go around the room and ask each person to comment on number 1 below, and then invite other team members to offer feedback and insight to their teammates. Then work to answer number 2 together as a team, determining next steps. Finally, be sure to review all these matters in your next team meeting, continuing to press forward.

1. Ask each person to answer the following questions.
- What's the most important thing you personally accomplished in the last week?
- What are the most important tasks or projects that you personally are working on this week?

- What potentially stands in the way of you personally accomplishing your work, and how can the team help you?

2. In light of and in pursuit of our team purpose,
- What's the most important thing we need to accomplish as a team this week?
- How can we best approach that work this week? (Think roles, assignments, communication, coordination, etc.)

You might ask these same questions in your regular meetings moving forward.

Before we go to the next step, we want to remind you about the necessity to continue developing psychological safety among your team (we first introduced the concept in step 3). Much has been said and written lately about the importance of psychological safety and how to cultivate it, but we'll boil it down for you. If you want to create a team with psychological safety—one in which team members respect and trust one another enough such that they will be vulnerable with one another, take appropriate risks, admit failures, and fully express themselves and their ideas and opinions—you need to[5]

> *Conflict is the fuel for great team performance. You must cultivate it.*

- Take risks yourself, even if they fail. When you do, you acknowledge that it is not only okay to risk and fail, but that doing so is expected on your team. (In fact, the reality is that "Real teams do not emerge unless the individuals on them take risks involving conflict, trust, interdependence and hard work.")[6]

- Treat people kindly, the way you would want to be treated. Some people call that being civil. Our world and your team could use more of it these days.

- Model and encourage pushback on one another's ideas. Conflict is the fuel for great team performance. You must cultivate it.

As you walk through Exercise 4.1, act in these ways, and encourage others to do the same.

STEP 17: DECIDE WHAT TO DO
COLLECTIVELY AND INDIVIDUALLY

Great teams engage both collective and individual work. Notice that Exercise 4.1 asks you and your team to address both collective and individual tasks. That's because collaborative teamwork is not always the best approach for a given task. Nor is individual action. You want to develop a rhythm of individual and then collective and then individual action (and it doesn't matter whether collective or individual action comes first, just that you engage both).

It's best to use a collaborative team approach when

- the task requires more resources than one person can offer
- diverse skills and perspectives are necessary to do the work
- flexibility and creativity are necessary to keep pace in your industry
- individuals can grow through engagement on the team and with its members

This also means that an individual approach may work better when

- the task is simple
- the task can be easily divided and conquered among team members
- one person's abilities far exceed that of the group
- speed is absolutely necessary (though speed is often unnecessarily prioritized)

As you look at the work your team must accomplish, determine what should be done individually and collectively. In short, if a team can't do it better than an individual, stick with the individual.

Warren, for example, has designed many research projects, from studying the latest trends in church planting to exploring best practices of effective church boards. While he has the skills and abilities to design surveys by

If a team can't do it better than an individual, stick with the individual.

himself, he never does. He always creates a team who then brings in diverse ideas, articulates various felt needs that warrant being researched, and helps him think out of the box. Without exception his survey ideas are dramatically improved. Those teams take what Warren could capably do alone and elevates it to a much higher level, all leading to superior outcomes.

Finally, the best teams spend most of their team meeting time deciding direction and coordinating activities rather than informing one another or advising the senior leader. Unfortunately, most teams do the opposite. Quickly consider the percentage of time in your team meetings that are devoted to

- making decisions or coordinating activities: ___%
- advising the senior leader or sharing information: ___%

Take an honest assessment. Then begin to structure your meetings to make important decisions together and coordinate your work (which often includes individual efforts). As you do, minimize taking time to simply inform people or, if you are the senior leader in a group, gather advice from your team. Inform or ask for advice via email, Slack, or one-on-one meetings. Then work together in your meetings by making decisions or managing interdependencies.

STEP 18: DEVELOP YOUR TEAM'S WORKING VALUES

Most likely, you've had some terrible team experiences (and maybe one or two good ones!). So has the rest of your team.

NOW IT'S YOUR TURN

Today's the day to take some time to mine those experiences for what's worked and what hasn't and establish some ground rules for how you'll work together now and into the future (see **Exercise 4.2**).

EXERCISE 4.2—Developing a list of your team's working values

1. Ask, What lights your fire? In other words, when working together in a team experience, what do you love?

2. Ask, What burns you up? What drives you crazy in team or group situations?

3. Mine these lists to develop a list of dos and don'ts for how you will work together as a team. Be sure to include the following elements:
- Meeting practices. What will regular meetings look like? Consider when you will have them, how long you will meet, and expectations for engagement.
- Communication expectations. Consider when and why you will use particular mediums, along with expectations for response based on medium.
- Interaction expectations. Discuss how you will communicate with one another, in what ways, how frequently, etc.

4. Finally, spend some time discussing an accountability framework. How will you respond if or when a team member violates the ground rules you've identified through this process?

5. Take a few minutes to document into your team charter (step 10) what you've developed.

STEP 19: CULTIVATE STORY-DRIVEN CAMARADERIE

There is one kind of team-building activity that drives enhanced team performance: knowing one another's stories as a way to deeply understand who team members are and how they roll (e.g., what motivates them, what concerns them, how they work, etc.).

Schedule some time today to create space where you can get to know one another better. You might schedule an off-site day to share your stories, or decide to add a half-hour to your next several weekly meetings—depending on the size of your team—to give one person each week a chance to tell their story.

Léonce thought he knew a good deal about most of his teammates because some of them had been with him since the prelaunch days of Renovation Church. But several years ago he took the executive leadership team on a retreat to do some team building and planning.

One of his friends, who is also a pastor in Atlanta, had suggested to Léonce, "Take some time to hear each other's stories. I cannot tell you how powerful and transformative it was for our team." There was no way Léonce could know how significant and bonding this exercise would be for their team.

Following that advice, the team took five or so hours to hear each other's stories. The things that surfaced ranged from incredibly hilarious to gut-wrenching and heartbreaking.

Many tears were shed that day, but when the team headed home a couple of days later, they left with a deeper sense of knowing each other, of empathy, and of excitement as a team.

If you need some help in crafting your story, consider the following frameworks.

1. Lay out key positive and negative experiences in your life (arranged vertically, depending on how high or low the experience is) across a chronological timeline of your life.

2. Map out chronologically key moments, including challenging, difficult moments, top-of-the-world moments, events that changed or shaped your life, poignant expressions of God's faithfulness in

your life, key people or relationships in your life, and decisions that have altered your life course.[7]

Using either of these frameworks, you will quickly get a sense of your life story, shaping moments, and turning points in your life. And when you share your stories with one another, you will find a deepening sense of commitment, understanding, and trust.

STEP 20: WRITE A MULTI-DIRECTIONAL USER MANUAL

Finally, building off your stories, take some time to ask each member of your team to write a two-page *Team Member User Manual* (see the template at www.resiliencefactor.info), which includes sections that address issues like

- work loves
- wiring
- strengths
- weaknesses
- preferred communication style
- feedback style and preferences
- pet peeves
- working-style values
- wounds
- energizers and deenergizers

Once each person crafts these, distribute the user manuals to your team members, giving each person a chance to talk through their manual and others the opportunity to ask clarifying questions. Then include them as attachments to your team charter.

■ ■ ■

You're at the halfway mark! Congratulations. You're halfway through your forty-step journey to a new team. And you've already taken several *huge* steps forward in building your team.

NOW IT'S YOUR TURN

Take a few minutes today to reflect on the ways your team has already grown (see **Exercise 4.3**).

. . . .

EXERCISE 4.3—Assessing our team's growth (in just four weeks)

1. We've already had some important conversations about . . .

2. We're already starting to do better with . . .

3. We've experienced some serious aha moments as a team, such as . . .

4. We're excited to keep growing as a team because . . .

Keep on working, pressing forward. And remember, as you do this sometimes hard work together, you are slowly and surely, bit by bit, building a team that will deeply trust one another. And as you do, you'll soon be able to face anything.

Movement five will help you design incredible meetings, the kind that people want to attend.

END-OF-CHAPTER SUMMARY AND ACTION ITEMS

If you forget everything else, remember this as your team gets to work and begins to develop in the process:

1. Build trust in the trenches, not in nonworking isolated exercises, because trust is a byproduct of the pursuit of shared purpose.

2. Actively delineate between tasks that are better handled by individuals and those tasks that are better addressed through collective efforts.

3. Mine how difficult team experiences can become fuel for shaping the values of a team you are excited to be on.

4. Engage your teammates' stories to get to know each of them better.

5. Write and share insights about you and how you work that will help your teammates better understand and get the most from you, and listen to your teammates do the same.

Reflection and Discussion Questions

1. What was the most useful or helpful insight you read in this movement?

2. Looking back over your experiences as a team, what experience or circumstance has yielded the greatest results in team building?

3. What tasks on your team will most benefit from a collaborative approach, as opposed to an individualistic approach?

4. At this moment, what difference do you think it is making for your teammate to have a better understanding of how one another works?

5. What did you do or learn this week that will be most useful to this team moving forward?

Take It Deeper

1. Invite one of your teammates to coffee and share how your teammate's story has affected you.

2. Invite your spouse, trusted mentor, counselor, or pastor to look over your user manual and give feedback based on how they experience you. Make adjustments based on your new insights.

3. Work on telling your story in a way that is honest, compelling, and vulnerable.

4. Move on to the next step, carrying with you the action steps you identified this week.

DESIGN KILLER MEETINGS (STEPS 21-25)

YOU CAN CREATE MEETINGS
YOUR TEAM ACTUALLY WANTS
TO ATTEND

LET'S FACE IT: for many, meetings are the bane of organizational life. They can be that painful last mile of a long run, sucking the air from your body and strength from your bones. They can lack focus, drone on for too long, or dwell on something different from the expressed purpose. Even with recent innovations such as stand-up meetings and specialized offsites, poor meetings plague both in-person and remote teams. But there's hope. You can experience intentional, productive, and enjoyable meetings where important decisions are made, bottlenecks are broken, and members feel like they've been good stewards of their time. In this chapter we'll help you create great meetings and, in the process, teach you a few techniques your team can use to make better group decisions, effectively solve problems, and develop innovative solutions to complex challenges.

W e're *done* with the never-ending process of planning and talking about things. I don't want to see you in each other's cubicles anymore; just get your work done!" the director barked one Monday, canceling all meetings for the week.

Strangely, people reacted by needing to raid the company kitchen more often and to take more breaks outside—where they just happened to bump into other people from their teams. "And we're not having a mail team either. If you walk by the front door and the mail just got delivered through the mail slot, then you be the one to deliver it," the director wrote in a memo to the twenty-five employees. This too didn't work, as most people started using the back door instead. The whole no-teams, no-meetings idea backfired, and the only person who had a good week was the director. But the employees secretly wondered if *he* got much work done!

Even so, it did shake everyone up to ask themselves, *Do we need these meetings, and could they get any better?* But they also concluded that they did need to work together at some level.

If it's true that teams that focus on performance "will deliver results well beyond what individuals working alone in non-team settings could achieve," then those teams must develop effective, meaningful rhythms of working together.[1] Meetings done right are one of the most effective tools your team has to do your work and pursue your purpose.

STEP 21: REPEATEDLY ASK THE SIMPLE QUESTION, WHY ARE WE MEETING?

One thousand eighty dollars. That's the approximate cost to your organization every month for a weekly ninety-minute meeting with six people who average $50,000 in salaries. That may not seem like a lot, but over a year, that's $13,000. But you know that your team members don't have just *one* meeting a week. Do some quick math and you'll see just how much meetings cost.[2] Then add to that the opportunity costs for what you and your team are *not* doing and the discouragement and energy drain resulting from so many meetings. It's not hard to see the potential downsides of every meeting someone convenes.

The first way to dramatically improve your meetings is to . . . wait for it . . . conduct meetings *only* when necessary. In other words, you should call a meeting only if it is the best option to get what you need to get done. Remember, the only reason to work as a team on a task is if the team can accomplish something better than individuals working on it alone.

Of course, that seems so simple, but the reality is that so many meetings—we suggest *most*—are not driven by that basic rule. Instead, leaders call meetings for all kinds of reasons other than to get things done that are best done by a group. Many meetings continue every week primarily because that's what's on the calendar. Others are called to make it appear that work is being done collaboratively—even when everyone there knows the key decisions have already been made or will be determined in a meeting *after* the meeting (or perhaps even a meeting *before* the meeting). Sometimes

> *You should call a meeting only if it is the best option to get what you need to get done.*

leaders call meetings to get an audience for their pet idea, to whine about something, to take a break from a difficult individual task, or even to bolster their fragile ego by exercising their power to force everyone to stop what they are doing for an hour and do what the leader says. Ouch!

When there are so many meetings, it's easy for your team members to feel like all they do is meet, never really finding the time to get work done.

The reality is that your organization likely does not need more committees, and usually you need fewer meetings as well.

Recently Léonce received a Slack message from one of Renovation Church's pastors, asking what Léonce believed to be the best time and format for a meeting of volunteers and parents. The other pastor followed the request with several clarifying questions: "Should it be in person or digital? Should we provide childcare? What about food?"

After Léonce read all the questions, he responded with one simple question of his own: "Is the meeting about information or transformation?"

There was a long pause before the next message arrived, to which the other pastor responded, "I am not yet sure." Léonce's response was kind but direct: "Answering that question will sort out whether the need is in person or digital."

Moments later the other pastor responded that he felt it was more about information, to which Léonce volleyed, "Then why do you need a meeting?"

Distributing updates and information does not require a meeting; there are many other communication mediums to get information into people's hands. Ultimately no meeting was called, an email was sent, some follow-up calls happened, and three hours and maybe $1,000 in food, printing, and childcare costs were saved.

"Why are we meeting?" or "Does this require a meeting?" must be the filter for determining how best to engage as a team. Many times a call, Slack message, or email will suffice.

Of course, there are also many good reasons to call meetings.

Team meetings should be called when (and only when) the meeting will help the team accomplish their team purpose, usually by

- making an important decision together
- coordinating their activities (at a level that is too complex to handle asynchronously through email or a channel like Slack)
- solving an important problem together
- ideating for future innovation
- celebrating an individual or team win

Unless a meeting is essential, kill it.

Certainly, those are good reasons to call a meeting. But notice what's not there: getting people on the same page, reviewing details that have previously been communicated through email or other means, or informing the team of organizational happenings.

So today, decide to regularly ask the question, Do we need a meeting for that? As you honestly voice this question, you'll begin to appraise your team's meeting rhythms and determine which meetings (or segments of meetings) are truly important and which can go.[3]

Our recommendation: Unless a meeting is essential, kill it. Or at the least, suspend it for a while. Trust us, you won't miss it for long.

STEP 22: CREATE DIFFERENT MEETINGS
FOR DIFFERENT PURPOSES

The most effective teams we've observed don't try to cram everything into one weekly meeting. Rather, they use different meetings for different purposes.

At one elder-led church in Los Angeles, the elders, some of whom are also staff pastors, join together for a weekly prayer meeting. In addition they hold a separate elders' meeting, during which the team provides updates on a segment of the church's members, makes strategic ministry decisions, and reviews key areas of ministry on a rotating basis. A different pastor leads a weekly weekend-services meeting, which involves most of the elders and the church's media director. Finally, the elders meet roughly once every other month for half-day planning meetings, during which they discuss philosophy of ministry, review doctrinal matters, plan strategic activities such as setting the annual budget, and so on.

All these meetings are carefully planned and executed so all of the relevant team members contribute and provide leadership to the congregation—but they don't try to do it all at the same time. Instead, they invite different elders and pastors to different meetings, ensuring the right people are in the room for the right tasks and topics, thus enabling those not as necessary to carry on with their regular work. This makes for highly effective and efficient meetings.

NOW IT'S YOUR TURN

Your team needs to consider different meetings for different purposes too. Use **Exercise 5.1** to take stock of your meetings and to determine a meeting rhythm that will serve you well.

· ·

EXERCISE 5.1—Developing different meetings for different purposes

1. On a whiteboard draw a different large circle for every recurring meeting your team holds (include weekly, monthly, quarterly, and annual meetings). In each circle list the tasks that typically get accomplished in each of these meetings.

2. Referring back to step 21, cross off all activities in those meetings that do not need to be accomplished in a meeting setting. You might realize you can kill some entire meetings. Congratulations!

3. Now, are there any items that would be better accomplished in a different meeting? If so, move those items to other meetings. Or consider bundling similar items that require the same people in them.

4. Finally, for each meeting you identify as essential, write a brief purpose statement for that meeting and a list of preferred attendees for each one.

5. Capture these meeting purpose statements and attendee lists in your team charter.

STEP 23: ELIMINATE DECISION-MAKING MEETINGS AFTER THE MAIN MEETING

If you want your entire team to take meetings seriously, you've got to do the toughest and most essential work within your meetings. That means you need to identify whether the real decisions are being made in another meeting and, if so, to talk about that elephant in the room. Some refer to this other meeting as the kitchen-cabinet meeting, a smaller meeting where the actual power brokers are talking. If you agree that the other-meeting practice is your reality, the next step is for the power brokers to agree that their current process is counterproductive; it's likely unempowering and discouraging for your team.

Of course, this process will require great candor, trust, and diplomacy. The transition of power works best in an environment of respect, kindness, and affirmation. The conversations must speak truth—but with love, as Scripture calls us to do (Ephesians 4:15). If there is a lack of respect or an unwillingness to delve into disquieting or uncomfortable areas, then this transfer of power is impossible. Wherever trust lacks, unhealthy assumptions and mistrust will flourish.

Wherever trust lacks, unhealthy assumptions and mistrust will flourish.

If you allow other meetings to do the real work (even if they're just quick conversations), you'll continue to get meeting attendees who either come unprepared or disengage throughout your meeting. Why? They believe that what they bring to the table doesn't matter, so they don't bring much.

One last note: a meeting after the meeting that debriefs a meeting—what went well and what could be improved—does have value. You don't need to kill that one. While we'd encourage you to do the debriefing with the whole team whenever possible, identifying ways a future meeting could be better is the kind of reflection your resilient team needs.

STEP 24: EMBRACE DISCOMFORT AND USE STRUCTURED DISCUSSION TECHNIQUES

Anyone who has ever followed a diet or workout plan knows the power of structure. Left on your own it's easy to be less disciplined than you wish to be. As a result, you don't see the gains or losses you wish to see.

Groups and teams suffer from the same problem. Without structure, groups tend to waste time and accomplish fewer of their objectives. Groups that do not structure their decision-making processes effectively tend to make less-than-stellar decisions because they

1. possess and work with too little or too much *information,*

2. fail to properly *analyze* the situation and the information they have available, and

3. live in a world of old solutions rather than a world of new *possibilities.*

But when they impose structure for making decisions, solving problems, or innovating new directions, good things tend to follow. They can deal well with the information they have, effectively analyze the problem, and envision previously unknown possibilities.

Just as setting relational boundaries feels awkward at the time, imposing structure by utilizing formal discussion procedures can feel a bit awkward at first. But the temporary discomfort in both of those settings pays long-term benefits in those relationships and teams.

We encourage you to impose structure in the following three key ways.

Manage your meetings better. First, use a routine standardized agenda with the same weekly discussion topics (e.g., important deadlines this week, updates on key initiatives, etc.) so people know what to expect in each meeting. Distribute it and any other preparatory reading at least two days in advance so that everyone comes well prepared.

Warren remembers a monthly Tuesday evening church board where at each gathering easily half of the meeting was spent looking up information or working together to try to remember details that the church's office manager could have found in seconds but only if asked that morning while she was still in the office. When Warren became board chair for a year, he began contacting the office manager or various members to ask what they could prepare for the meeting. "We'll be talking this Tuesday about playground upgrades. Could you find a list of repairs and costs from the last couple of years?" The culture change was uphill and not easy (because the pastor was just fine with a no-preparation approach), but each time everyone came prepared with relevant information, the meetings were faster, happier, and more effective.

By contrast, much preparation goes toward board meetings at Warren's current employer, ECFA. A full week before the meeting, each board member receives a well-organized PDF that starts with the agenda and then offers relevant background information on each point to be discussed. The high expectation that board members will come to the meeting prepared is conveyed. As a result the meetings are efficient and effective and allow space for fun as the board members work together.

Don't be afraid to allow others to contribute to building your meeting agenda, but appoint someone to drive the ship. Someone needs to determine what makes the agenda and time devoted to each item, reorder the agenda to put the weightiest issues near the front, and identify procedures that will be used to accomplish each item.

Once you get into your meeting, actually follow the agenda in your meeting, creatively determining how you will accomplish each agenda item (using techniques like those that follow).

Finally, ensure everyone takes their action or homework notes (instead of or in addition to a notetaker).

Solve problems and make better decisions. In most cases teams make much better decisions than individuals acting alone, given the greater information available among the various team members, the benefits afforded by multiple experiences, knowledge, and perspectives, and the critical thinking fostered when team members wrestle with the assumptions and alternatives that drive decisions. But often teams do not make better decisions precisely because they don't engage in a way that enables the team to adequately handle the sheer amount of information available to them, and they fail to engage the critical analysis that leads to outstanding decisions. Thus, with some additional structure, you can make it easy for your team to take the necessary steps to make better decisions.

Here are two tools you can use to impose more structure on how you solve problems and make decisions as a team.

The functional decision-making approach. One easy method for making better decisions is called a functional decision-making approach.[4] In general better decisions are made when groups attend to the following five functions:

1. Analyze the problem, determining the nature, source, extent, and seriousness of the issue you are engaging in.

2. Establish criteria against which you can evaluate possible solutions, setting specific standards that the final choice must satisfy to be judged acceptable.

3. Generate alternative solutions to solve the problem at hand, working to creatively identify as many solutions (different, out-of-the-box, beyond-current-practice) as possible.

4. Evaluate the positive and negative consequences of the solutions identified in function 3, perhaps by discussing the pros and cons of each possible solution against the criteria set in function 2.

5. Finally, select a course of action judged most likely to satisfy the standards identified in function 2.

The devil's advocacy approach. Another great structured approach to making better decisions is the devil's advocacy technique. In this process a group is split into two subgroups, one group develops a solid argument *for* a recommended course of action while the other plays devil's advocate and formally *critiques* that recommendation. The group goes through a few rounds of presentation and critique until both groups agree that the recommended course of action is suitable for implementation.[5] Figure 5.1 outlines the basic framework.

The beauty of this technique is that (1) it will help you make a more thoughtful, informed decision that your entire team buys into; (2) it permits quiet members to disagree (even aggressively); and (3) it teaches your entire team to offer strong arguments in response to critique.

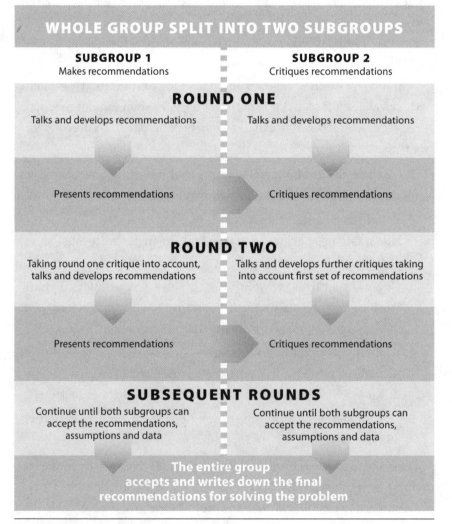

Figure 5.1. Basic framework of the devil's advocacy approach

Practice this technique (or even the spirit it represents) and you'll get a better decision today and a stronger decision-making team tomorrow.

No matter what you do, be sure to practice these key principles to increase the quality of your group decision-making.

- Don't just share your perspective. Ask for others' thoughts and information.

- Ensure that everyone speaks, shares what they know, and offers their input.

- If you're the formal leader who is often offered deference by team members, speak last (especially if you know that you'll shut down further conversation once you enter the conversation).

- Manage "conversation hogs" to create space for quieter members.

- Invite everyone to make strong, compelling arguments in support of suggested directions as well as thoughtful, nuanced critiques of others' ideas.

- Cultivate a norm of *If you see something, say something.*

At one church he served, Warren looked forward to the board meetings because he learned so much! One board member worked with the pastor before the meeting to help each agenda item have a laser focus on the area where the board needed to weigh in or be aware. Another board member regularly tinkered with the church's software, bringing amazing dashboard insights to the meetings. Another person verbally called out "we're in the weeds!" when board discussions tilted into inappropriate micromanagement. Those meetings hopped with focus, efficiency, and many fun moments along the way! That board team consistently made superior decisions.

Identify and develop new, creative ideas. Most likely your team is not as creative as it could be. Even if you regularly follow the rules of brainstorming, you likely are leaving creative potential on the table. Here are a few tips to better identify and develop new, creative ideas.

- Live in the land of interests (what you want) instead of positions (ways to get what you want). Using a simple example, if you want to find a creative lunch option, consider interests (cost, location, noise level, allergy accommodations, etc.) instead of positions (the chain Mexican joint, the burger bar, or the local diner). Considering your interests will open a new world of possibilities.

- Delay critique of ideas. Get them all on the table before you discuss their relative merits or disadvantages (waiting to cheer or jeer ideas is difficult and quite unnatural).

- Reduce turn-taking times by letting everyone ideate simultaneously. If you are listing ideas, appoint two scribes to alternate writing down ideas so that the group doesn't have to slow down while one scribe writes, ask people to write down their ideas while listening to others' input, and alternate between individual and group engagement.

- Emphasize piggybacking on ideas, but don't get stuck for too long on one train of thought. Because people are generally more creative together than apart, find ways to get one another to hear—and be inspired by—one another's ideas. However, if the ideas stagnate for too long, change course dramatically to stimulate new ideas.

- Encourage combinations of ideas. Sometimes you'll find a great innovative idea from one person's complete thought, but often you'll be looking for the *aha!* moment when several people's ideas are combined into a beautiful, workable solution.

Our favorite tool to quickly generate a lot of ideas is the *lotus blossom technique*. Here's how to generate a ton of ideas super quickly.

1. Give each member a stack of Post-it Notes, and head to a wall.

2. On one Post-it Note, write the issue about which you want to generate new ideas (e.g., ways to celebrate volunteers), and stick it to the middle of the wall.

3. Then, encourage each person to write an idea (or two) related to the issue on a Post-it Note and stick it around the first note—in any order. See figure 5.2. Do not critique or comment on the ideas at this stage.

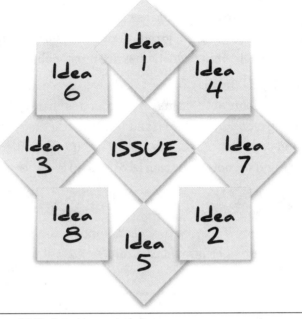

Figure 5.2. The lotus blossom technique

4. Then, unfold the blossom by grabbing any one of the idea notes (e.g., sending a coffee gift card) and placing it in a blank area of the wall. Anyone can grab any other note and move it out on the wall, creating space to surround that idea with Post-it Notes highlighting other new ideas that are inspired by that one (e.g., a fun box of goodies, a group trip to Starbucks, or anything else inspired by that idea). This repeats the previous step of the process, surrounding each of the copied idea notes with secondary ideas, using only the copied idea notes as stimuli. You can create and unfold blossoms as many times as you like.

5. Soon, you'll have 8–10 blossoms around the room and 80–100 ideas on the wall, in a matter of minutes. If your group doesn't move around and contribute to all the blossoms naturally, you can rotate them around the lotus, asking each person to put a secondary idea onto a copied idea and then move on to the next copied idea. Don't worry about duplicate ideas; just get as many ideas on the board as possible.

6. From there, if you want to begin to identify the best ideas of those generated, you could ask each person to select two or three of their favorite ideas, group them, and then discuss them as a group to determine which ones are most viable and impactful.

This tool levels the playing field and gives everyone on your team a chance to contribute at the same time, generates energy among the team, allows for piggybacking of ideas, and then sets the stage for further discussion and consideration of key ideas. Give it (or another similar technique) a try and see how your team all of sudden becomes quite creative.[6]

NOW IT'S YOUR TURN

Do it! Even though it may be awkward, impose some structure that improves your team's performance.[7] **Exercise 5.2** will help you try a new technique.

••

EXERCISE 5.2—Trying a new technique

1. Pick a problem you need to solve, a decision you need to make, or a topic that needs creative ideas.

2. Go to *The Resilience Factor* book website (www.resiliencefactor.info), pick a discussion technique to use, download the tool, and work through it with your team.

3. Afterward, discuss how the technique helped you accomplish your objective.
  • What felt awkward or forced?
  • What did your team do differently using this procedure?
  • Were you able to accomplish your objective:
    – more effectively?
    – more quickly?
    – with more input?
  • What would you add or take away from the technique you chose?

STEP 25: FOLLOW THROUGH BETWEEN MEETINGS

If the activities of steps 21–24 become your ongoing practice, you will have taken massive steps to improve your team meetings. People will know their contributions matter, so they'll show up more prepared and engage more fully. That will result in better decisions made as you accomplish your objectives together, pursuing your team's unique purpose. And your team members will be energized and will look forward to showing up the next time. You'll build a snowball of growing engagement, enjoyment, and effectiveness in your meetings. That's a good thing.

But there's one more thing you've got to do—follow through.

Unfortunately, this is where too many teams falter. They show up for the big game but then don't follow through on what they've decided and delegated.

> *Make a list of who's doing what and by when.*

But not you. In every meeting, each team member must follow through. Here's what that looks like.

1. Toward the end of your meeting, discuss what each person in the room is doing before your next meeting. (Even if you have someone take minutes, ensure that all participants know what they are accountable for. The first few times, the meeting facilitator may need to keep a running list to fill in if participants forget what they need to do.)

2. Communicate frequently on those deliverables and action items. Do this through tools like Slack, email threads, and pop-in discussions.

3. Well before your next meeting, send out an agenda that reflects (and reminds) the action items established in the previous meeting.

Lather, rinse, repeat. And watch your meetings transform from a necessary evil of group life to one of the most effective, action-oriented times for your team each week or month.

We used that approach in writing this book. Our team of three people, living in different cities, each with a very different job rhythm, needed to make a list on each weekly call of who's doing what and by when. And each week one of us gathered the various weekly accomplishments and initiatives into an agenda for our weekly call.

■ ■ ■

All of this work is not only helping your team get better but also developing the members of your team into stronger, more capable leaders. Movement six addresses how to turn your team into a powerful leadership development incubator.

END-OF-CHAPTER SUMMARY AND ACTION ITEMS

If you forget everything else, remember this as you work to develop amazing meetings:

1. Carefully consider the various costs of meetings, and ensure that you have a clear purpose for every meeting you call.

2. Don't try to do it all in one meeting. Instead, establish different meetings for different purposes, with different participants, to drive different results.

3. Do the thorniest, real work in your actual team meetings, not in another meeting of a small group before or after.

4. Embrace the awkward and structure your meetings, decision-making processes, and creativity sessions to get more of what you want.

5. Follow through after your meetings so you execute and create momentum on your key initiatives.

Reflection and Discussion Questions

1. What was the most useful or helpful insight you read in this movement?

2. In what ways are your meetings strong right now, and in what ways do your meetings have the most potential for improvement?

3. On a scale of 1 (low) to 10 (high), how *killer* are your meetings at present? What would it take to move them to at least an 8, if they're not that high already?

4. What did you do or learn this week that will be most useful to this team moving forward?

5. How do you carry forward what you learned here?

Take It Deeper

1. Go to *The Resilience Factor* website (www.resiliencefactor.info) and review several of the discussion procedures outlined there. Identify a meeting task that could be handled with one of those procedures, and then try it out.

2. Ask a trusted friend about the top two or three practices they use to run great meetings, and then try one out.

3. Clarify the purpose of every meeting you go to over the next three weeks and see what you learn from that process.

4. Move on to the next step, carrying with you the action steps you identified this week.

SHARPEN YOUR TEAM (STEPS 26-30)

YOUR TEAM CAN SERVE AS A POWERFUL LEADERSHIP DEVELOPMENT INCUBATOR

MANY TEAM MEMBERS FEEL undervalued and uncared for at a personal level. The demands of leadership require fast action and constant innovation, leaving little room to focus on people development. But ultimately both business and ministry is all about people, and teams done right are one of the greatest leadership development incubators. In this chapter we cast a vision for ongoing individual investment and team development and lay out several strategies that will sharpen the skill sets of team members and increase feelings of appreciation, satisfaction, and loyalty among your team members.

Whether you are a college football fan or not, the name Nick Saban likely rings a bell. Like him or not, Coach Saban has cemented himself as the greatest college football coach of the modern era and perhaps of all time.

For those of you who are football fans, you may think this designation as the greatest coach is related to his many conference wins. Or his national championships, which he has dominated for a decade.

But Nick Saban's greatest achievement as a head coach is not related to the championship teams he produced. Instead, it is in the leaders that were incubated on his coaching staff.

As of this publication, seven former Nick Saban assistant coaches are head coaches of NCAA Power Five programs, the largest and most elite level of college football. But when you dig deeper, you will find that Saban's staff teams have produced twenty-four—*twenty-four*—head coaches across the country, at every level of the game.

Teams done right produce more than great results or big wins. They produce able leaders who, when the time is right, go on to lead at the highest level themselves.

If Nick Saban's coaching tree is any indication of what is possible, then a great team atmosphere—one that serves as an incubator for developing leaders—can easily have national, even global, implications. But early on you must ensure your team focuses on building leaders, both for now and for the future.

STEP 26: DEFINE *LEADERSHIP* AND THEN ASSESS YOUR OWN LEADERSHIP

Definitions matter. A lot. The way you think about anything affects how you *see* and *practice* that thing. For instance, the way you define the essence of marriage—as a partnership between two people for as long as they agree to abide by it versus as a covenantal, sacrificial, lifelong relationship—will dramatically affect how you *do* marriage. The way you *think* influences what you *do*.

So it is for leadership.

The question, therefore, is what does leadership mean in *your* context? If you've never taken time to wrestle with what constitutes leadership for your team or organization, you'll struggle to effectively develop leaders. Because you haven't agreed on what leadership is, it's impossible to know what a leader looks like. But as soon as you define the target—what *good* leadership looks like in your context—you'll be able to identify those who are doing it and 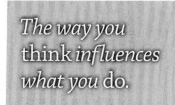 those who work to do it more effectively, and then take meaningful action to grow the capacity of every member of your team to lead better and with more impact.

At one point Warren was leading a five-person team in a nonprofit ministry. He met one-on-one weekly with each person, but they never met as a full team. At the time Warren (wrongly) didn't think that was necessary since he was the assignment giver and they were the doers. At the time, leadership for Warren meant being a good manager: making all the big decisions himself and helping each staff member execute them well. Any development occurred by Warren learning to improve his assignment-giving abilities and the staff becoming better doers. Hmm!

Money became tight for the ministry, and Warren had to let two of the people go. Yet the overall workload for his department remained the same. Warren asked each of the three remaining people if they were willing to take more leadership responsibility, to grow personally in their initiative and abilities, and to work more collaboratively with each other. They all genuinely and enthusiastically agreed.

Warren began to alternate his one-on-one meetings with meetings of the four-person team. Team members began to interact with each other independently of Warren. Everyone successfully rose to new challenges and somehow the workload was met. Looking back, each person today would say that they developed professionally at new levels, their capacity increased during that period, and their impact as a team grew.

So, to revisit the opening question, How do you define the words *leader* and/or *leadership* in your context?

The leadership team at Renovation Church has identified a few criteria by which they define a leader and leadership. Leadership in their context is a clear vision coupled with concrete faith and the will to execute. Further, they define a leader in their rubric of three Hs and five Selfs. The three Hs are *honest, hungry,* and *humble.* They believe that a leader must embody these character traits to effectively lead. The five Selfs, on the other hand, are not about character but drive. A leader is *self-aware, self-starting, self-encouraging, self-motivating,* and *self-correcting.* All who actively embody and grow in these Selfs will be effective leaders.

NOW IT'S YOUR TURN

Exercise 6.1 will help you define leadership, using Scripture as a guide.

....

EXERCISE 6.1—Defining leadership

What is leadership? Develop your own definition and give reasons for it. Come prepared to share it with the group. The following prompts will help you develop your definition.

1. Consider what Scripture says about leadership. As two starting points, look up Matthew 20:25-28 and 1 Peter 5:1-6. What is essential for leadership?

2. Consult your favorite authors or thinkers on leadership. What do they say that resonates with you?

3. Armed with that background, succinctly state five activities or attitudes that leadership involves (such as serving others, influencing others, etc.).

4. Finally, write your brief definition of leadership.

If you need an example, Ryan developed the following definition over many years.

> (Biblical) Leadership is a positive, invitational, and ethical process of influencing followers to accomplish good, life-giving goals while also humbly shepherding, serving, and developing those followers.

Note that this definition sets a high bar for what counts as leadership. Does yours? Remember, the way you think affects how you do. If you set a low bar for leadership (for instance, leadership is simply influence), then you (and your team) won't be challenged to lead at a higher level. We urge you to elevate your definition of leadership and set a bar that will propel your leadership and leadership growth forward.

Once you've defined what good leadership means for you in your context, it's time to look in the mirror and take the time to assess yourself—and only yourself—against that definition. No matter whether you are the designated team leader or not, you have the potential to provide leadership. So, take stock: Where are you succeeding, and in what ways are you struggling?

NOW IT'S YOUR TURN

Don't worry about how others frame leadership at this point. Right now, assess yourself honestly against your definition. Take some time now to evaluate your leadership. Within your current role on your team, in what ways are you strong and in what areas do you have room to grow (see **Exercise 6.2**)?

. . . .

EXERCISE 6.2—Analyzing the strengths and weaknesses of my leadership

1. My key strengths:

2. My key weaknesses:

STEP 27: DECIDE AS A TEAM WHAT *LEADERSHIP* AND *LEADERS* LOOK LIKE IN YOUR CONTEXT

NOW IT'S YOUR TURN

Now work together to develop (1) a baseline agreement on what leadership means in your team context as well as (2) a list of what an effective leader looks like and does (see **Exercise 6.3**). As you wrestle through these conversations, you'll develop clarity on how you can develop one another's leadership capacity.

EXERCISE 6.3—Defining leadership together

1. Share with one another your individually developed definitions of leadership (developed in **Exercise 6.1**). As each is read, note commonalities as well as insights that resonate with you.

2. Work together to develop a brief statement that encapsulates a definition of leadership every member of your team can buy into. There's no need to get super specific. Consider framing it as follows:

For our _____ team,

effective leadership is _____
(think about processes and actions)

that _____
(think about effects and outcomes).

3. In line with that definition, list five to eight attributes and skills that leaders in your context should be and should be able to do.

Leaders here will . . .

(BE—think character)

(DO—think skill and ability)

4. Write your definition of leadership and a list of leader attributes and skills in your team charter.

Congratulations, you have established a target for leadership development.

STEP 28: ENGAGE IN HONEST CONVERSATIONS AS YOU ASSESS YOUR LEADERSHIP

Now that you've looked at yourself as a leader and now that you've established, as a team, what leadership means for your team, you are ready to engage with others, acknowledging your strengths and struggles and helping others to do the same. This is where the development begins and where that team psychological safety and trust that you've been building will pay huge dividends. If you haven't begun to develop a strong sense of safety among your team (though we've tried our darndest to invite you into the kinds of honest and challenging conversations that cultivate it), being honest is going to be hard.

Quite frankly, even if you sense a degree of psychological safety developing among your team, this next step is going to be challenging. But remember that you're doing this so you'll build the resilience you'll need to face anything together. So, step in boldly.

How do you offer feedback to one another successfully?

Start with strengths. Be specific about the good things people are bringing to the team, backed with real evidence. Affirm what you see in others. We suggest you do this in front of each other because it can be powerful. When you praise your teammates, consider their

1. Task competencies—what do they *do* well?

2. Team competencies—how do they *powerfully contribute* to your team?

3. Personal competencies—what about their *person* and *contribution* are particularly special or effective?

Two particularly effective ways to do this are to (1) set each team member in the hot seat, and then one by one go around the room praising that person, or (2) for each team member to post one sheet of flip-chart paper on the wall, and then give everyone markers and time to walk around the room and write specific praises on each person's paper. Both of these approaches are superior to sharing these strengths in private because they allow other team members to eavesdrop on the compliments offered, building a greater appreciation for each person.

Say even more about strengths. Most people benefit greatly from hearing multiple words about what they do well and where they're appreciated as making a difference. Make sure you have far more to say, and genuinely so, about the positives before you move to the next point.

At a different time, move to growth opportunities. Do this individually. The hot seat doesn't work here. Instead, invite team members to privately share areas for growth with one another, either by creating space for those conversations to happen throughout the week or by writing private notes to one another.

Whatever method you use, be sure to talk about behaviors rather than essences, offering examples of specific situations and what could be done differently or better. Don't use a compliment-sandwich approach—positive feedback followed by the real issue, followed by positive feedback—because merging positive and negative feedback is confusing. Stick to growth opportunities, perhaps helping others see how they can utilize their strengths to grow in those areas.

Ask the team for help. After each team member has been able to process their feedback, ask each person to answer this question before the group: "How can we help accentuate your strengths and minimize your weaknesses?" For instance, in a meeting Susanna says, "Based on the feedback I've received over the last week, here are some ways that you can help me build on and use my strengths and minimize my weaknesses." Of course, this is a good time to bring the *Team Member User Manual* back out and make adjustments based on this feedback.

For sure, this approach requires and results in a greater sense of humility. As one pastor told us, "If your ambition and desire to see the church grow is driving you, things like team will get in the way of your true ambition, but if you desire to know God, you will know his humility, and then it becomes so easy to submit as part of a team."

So, today, plan how you will engage in these conversations and assess one another.

STEP 29: PRIORITIZE REGULAR TEAM DEVELOPMENT

Now it's time to create customized development opportunities based on what you unearth in your conversations about how it is going.

Here are several ways to build team development into your regular work schedule and your regular work meetings. Which one would work best for the current circumstances of your team?

1. Read one article each week (or month) as a team and then discuss it for ten minutes at your regular team meeting. See our website www.resiliencefactor.info for a running list of great articles that will help you and your team develop.

2. Read through one to three books a year as a team, discussing them a chapter or two at a time.

3. Rotate the responsibility to bring a fifteen-minute skill advancement mini-seminar to various meetings. Topics could range from "how to gather better project feedback" to "how to make better decisions" to "five ways to get more out of Slack."

4. Attend a virtual conference together in place of or in addition to your regular meeting.

5. Listen to a leadership podcast together and discuss how the core learnings can make a difference in each individual and in the team.

6. Invite an expert to guide your team through a personality, leadership, or work-style testing tool.

The key is to make development a normal part of your routine so that it is not an add-on to what you are already doing.

May 2019 marked one year from the point at which Léonce's Renovation Church elder team grew from five to fourteen. Simply adding that many people to any team can easily create tension, internal struggle, factionalism, and gridlock. Add in some type-A personalities and you can see why Léonce and his elder team were courting disaster. To head off as much of the brewing chaos as they possibly could, Léonce decided to host a retreat and take the team through intensive Enneagram training.[1] The training was not only exceptional for each elder and spouse but also incredibly clarifying for their team.

The training gave language to many of the tensions the team had experienced over the previous year and helped the team see how the members' wounding, which showed up in each person's particular Enneagram profile, contributed so much to how each person engaged with the team. It was profound.

It would be nice to say that clarity led to total team cohesion, but it didn't. However, the clarity gained through that learning process led some members to eventually self-select off the team, allowing those remaining on the team to function and perform at a higher level and as a more cohesive unit.

STEP 30: INVITE OTHERS TO OBSERVE AND PARTICIPATE WITH YOUR TEAM

Finally, bring others into your team as one-time guests. Show them how you roll, even when your team isn't perfect. If you consistently do the things we've described in this chapter, your team will grow, and others will see the way your team is growing and the process that growth requires.

Your team doesn't have to have it all together. It will be better if you don't. At any time, bring people in to (1) advise you on a decision you are making, (2) contribute to a planning or brainstorming session, (3) observe and give feedback on how you navigate complex decisions, or (4) alert you to any overlapping plans being carried out by *other* teams.

Consider today who you can invite to join your team (temporarily) either to observe or participate in your important work. When you do this, you'll expose your current team to new ideas and insights, and you'll give those outside your team a chance to learn from your team. And you'll press your team to continually develop your resilience as you seek to share it with others.

■　■　■

When you take these five steps outlined in this movement, your team will become a leadership incubator, and you'll begin to cascade the impact of your team throughout your organization. Movement seven will help you develop manageable and meaningful accountability within and beyond your team.

END-OF-CHAPTER SUMMARY AND ACTION ITEMS

If you forget everything else, remember this as you grow your team into a powerful force for leadership development:

1. Clearly define what *leadership* means for you, and then regularly assess yourself against your definition.

2. Agree as a team on who leaders are, what they do, and what leadership looks like in your unique context.

3. Practice radical candor as you engage in encouraging and challenging conversations with your teammates.

4. Constantly pursue leadership development—one article, book, conference, or coach at a time.

5. Invite others into your team gatherings to spur your growth as well as the growth of those occasional contributors.

Reflection and Discussion Questions

1. What was the most useful or helpful insight each of you read in this movement?

2. How has your team (or another team in our organization) typically thought about how leaders are best developed, and how does this chapter support or challenge those views?

3. At this moment, what excites each of you most about turning your team into a powerful leadership development incubator?

4. What did you do or learn this week that will be most useful to this team moving forward?

5. How do you carry forward what you learned here?

Take It Deeper

1. Ask one or more trusted mentors where they see gaps in your leadership and its development. Perhaps even ask them to assess you in reference to your definition of leadership.

2. Choose one of the five Selfs (from Léonce's example) in which you need the most growth, and make a plan to develop that area.

3. Pick one course or conference you will attend within the calendar year that will help to shore up gaps in your leadership.

4. Move on to the next step, carrying with you the action steps you identified this week.

PURSUE MEANINGFUL ACCOUNTABILITY (STEPS 31-35)

YOU CAN CRAFT A MORE MEANINGFUL TEAM SCORECARD

TOO MANY ASSESSMENT ACTIVITIES don't result in data-informed change, and they often take too much work for so little impact. But assessment doesn't have to be that way. You can measure your team's progress in both meaningful and manageable ways. This chapter develops a framework for team assessment (in terms of both team process and outcomes) so that teams can measure what matters and also continuously improve.

Before each new ministry year, the Renovation Church leadership team gathers the members of the church to share the next year's ministry calendar. As 2021 ended, the team did just that, gathering the members for a meal and casting a vision for the next year.

As they walked through the calendar, covering everything from future member meals to church-hosted conferences, a young woman raised her hand. She politely asked, "What about the single folks in the church? Do we get a conference?"

In their planning of the conferences for that next year—marriage, leadership, and student conferences—the team had failed to plan any specific opportunity to equip the unmarried members of the church.

Though stunned at first by their oversight, Léonce recalls that the team rebounded, apologized, and then asked that young woman and several other single leaders in the church to hold them accountable and help them shape a singles conference.

Just a few months later, in March 2022, a team of nine unmarried people, both men and women, planned Renovation's first-ever singles conference. It was a huge success!

Had it not been for a culture of receptivity and accountability, this significant event—which led to several new people joining the church—would have never happened.

This chapter helps your team cultivate a culture and practice of meaningful accountability, both for your team and spilling out into your organization.

STEP 31: DEVELOP TEAM GOALS ENABLING YOU TO ACCOMPLISH YOUR 5C PURPOSE

If you haven't yet established a few team-level goals, now is the time to do so. Invite God into the process of establishing your team's objectives, and watch him show up.[1]

Effective team goals flesh out the team's overarching purpose or mission, for "a team's purpose and performance goals go together."[2] In other words, if your team accomplishes its goals, it should be fulfilling its purpose. (This is a good time to review that 5C purpose [see step 9].) Your performance goals transform the broad purpose into specific and mea-

> *When you accomplish your team's performance goals, you will know your team is fulfilling its mission.*

surable performance challenges. When you accomplish your team's performance goals, you will know your team is fulfilling its mission. In fact, "the most important characteristic of a high-performance team is that its members are clear about the team's goals . . . and members agree with the team goals."[3]

Set a few goals that balance long-term strategy with short-term execution. Effective teams both articulate long-term (multiyear) strategic goals and spark immediate action with short-term (next week or month) goals. Map your short-term objectives to long-term goals and watch the momentum grow!

As you develop your goals, use the SMART goal framework, which encourages specificity and measurability, enabling you to know if you are achieving your goals or just spinning your wheels.[4]

SMART GOALS

Specific. Define the who, what, where, and when with precision. You must know, exactly, what you are attempting to do and who is responsible to make it happen.

Measurable. Articulate precise criteria for assessment at particular time intervals. At first glance, it might be difficult to measure your goal, but if you stick with it, you'll likely find a way to measure what you are trying to accomplish.

Attainable. Ensure this is something your team actually can do. If the goal is too hard, you'll likely grow discouraged, but if it is too easy, your team will slack off.

Relevant. Make sure the goal matters, that by doing it you accomplish your team's unique purpose and serve the mission of the organization. Just because you can measure it doesn't mean you should pursue it.

Time-bound. Give yourself a deadline. On this date (make sure your goal is specific and measurable), you'll know if you reached your goal or not.

Example: Rather than saying, "We need to increase the number of leaders serving in children's ministry," a related SMART goal could be, "Our goal is to recruit an additional fifteen children's ministry leaders who will sign up to work at least two Sundays during February."

Finally, ensure that you frame your goals as team goals, not individual goals. Effective team goals require interdependence and limit divide-and-conquer behavior. In other words, they must not be goals that a person could accomplish alone, nor can they be goals that can be accomplished by simply adding the contributions of various team members. Dividing and conquering is one of the great enemies of teamwork, because it diminishes true teamwork to simply stapling together a bunch of individual efforts. If a task is so simple it can be accomplished by one person or by adding the contributions of several people (like aggregate sales goals for a bunch of independent salespeople), don't try to make it a team effort.

> *If a task is so simple it can be accomplished by one person or by adding the contributions of several people, don't try to make it a team effort.*

When you set great goals for your team, you'll garner commitment from every member of the team. You know a good team goal when each team member is fiercely committed to it. Not only do team members talk regularly about the team's goals among themselves, but they also easily recite them to people not on the team, and they take personal responsibility to see them accomplished.

NOW IT'S YOUR TURN

Take some time to develop two or three team goals that will focus your efforts over the next three months in **Exercise 7.1**, and then enter your key team goals in your team charter.

....

EXERCISE 7.1—Developing your team goals

In your next team meeting, establish up to three team goals using the SMART framework.

STEP 32: LIMIT WHAT YOU MEASURE AND
HOW LONG YOU MEASURE IT

What you measure matters. But when you try to measure too much, your focus is sent in too many different directions. You end up chasing metrics rather than achieving important mission-focused objectives. You end up studying to pass the test rather than learning.

That's why the best organizations and teams, even though they are data-informed, limit what they measure.[5] You should too. To develop a meaningful plan for the assessment of your team's objectives and growth, start first by focusing on one or two key outcomes, and then offer a reasonable level of autonomy in achieving those outcomes.

Studies show that employees who are given autonomy over how to achieve objectives outperform those who are micromanaged.[6] Sometimes objectives are driven by a linear process such as following a sales funnel, but in most other cases a sense of autonomy in approaching the work is crucial to fully engage teammates. Rather than control how your team members do their *tasks*, establish a goal and allow them to choose how to best get to that *goal*. This paradigm is particularly important with millennials and Gen Z.

At the same time don't ignore key activities that drive important results. In a business there might be a direct correlation between the number of outbound cold calls your sales representatives make and the number of deals closed each month. In that case you want to measure one or two fulcrum activities that drive your business results.

In addition to identifying one or two fulcrum activities, you and your team must be able to distinguish between lead and lag measures.[7] *Lag* measures are results. They help you measure what outcomes have been achieved. Thus, lag measures involve metrics like how many people came to church, how many gave, and what percentage served.

By contrast, *lead* measures are the levers you apply to influence the lag measures. These might include the number of brochures mailed, the type and quality of recruitment campaigns, classes offered, response time to inquiries, and so on. In other words, lead measures usually measure the activities that result in your lag measures. Lead measures matter mostly because of how they impact lag measures.

As you determine what you measure, focus on both lag and lead measures. Make sure you know what your key outcomes are (lag measures). But also spend time thinking about a few key processes and actions (lead measures) that you believe will influence that goal. And regularly measure your progress on those lead measures so you can see what is making a difference in one way or another.

Whatever you do, don't focus on too many metrics, which will ultimately dilute your focus. We suggest prioritizing three or four metrics at a time, even though some teams that operate in particularly complex contexts, such as executive leadership teams, might extend beyond that number.

Develop a data dashboard, a way to visually show regularly the progress your team has made on your goals. Managers of fundraising campaigns tend to do this well, regularly indicating how much cash has been raised against the goal in a graphically appealing manner. Other team leaders need to follow their lead. Even if you're measuring leadership capability on ten competencies (such as those you developed in step 23), you can capture data and present it in a way that allows your team to see reality and where progress is still needed. Use what works for you: pie charts showing percentages, bar graphs indicating numbers, and so forth. But do *something* to show how well your team is doing.

> *Focus on both lag and lead measures.*

Dave Ferguson and Warren Bird's book *Hero Maker* is a study of lead measures that drive lag measures.[8] Everyone wants to help form leaders who in turn develop other leaders. That's the lag measure. But how? The book explains five lead measures, from giving I-C-N-U (I see in you . . .) affirmations to developing an apprentice culture. They basically assert, if you want more leaders, here are ways to develop them.

NOW IT'S YOUR TURN

As you work on lead and lag measures (see **Exercise 7.2**), consider shorter sprints on goals. Rather than assessing your performance once each year, cut down your time frame to two to three months. Paying attention at shorter intervals pushes innovation and enables teams to make faster adjustments that drive different results. Focusing on shorter intervals also minimizes the inevitable mission drift that surfaces, which must be resisted, in every organizational culture.

....

EXERCISE 7.2—Distinguishing between key lag and lead measures

List what you would nominate as your team's top two lag measures. Then list two lead measures that significantly contribute to each one.

Lag measure 1:

Lead measures:

1.

2.

Lag measure 2:

Lead measures:

1.

2.

Where are you strongest? Which of your lead measures need the most attention?

STEP 33: CULTIVATE MUTUAL ACCOUNTABILITY
FOR INDIVIDUAL DELIVERABLES

The basic rhythm of performance management is (1) setting goals and objectives, (2) tracking progress, and (3) providing feedback and coaching.[9] Often a manager works with an individual employee on this cycle, conducting performance reviews on a regular schedule (annually, quarterly, etc.). However, with resilient teams the entire team is best engaged in this process.

Here's how you can utilize your entire team in this process.

1. *Setting individual performance objectives.* Develop each person's objectives for the next period in a team meeting. Ask each person to share their tentative goals, and then request feedback from the team.

2. *Tracking individual and team progress.* Once each person has documented their goals, ask them to post them in conspicuous places so that your team constantly sees them. If you have a conference room where the team often meets, post them on the wall. In addition, start each meeting by having one person write their goals on a flip chart or whiteboard, explain their progress to the team, and then ask for feedback.

3. *Offering feedback and coaching.* Ask each team member to regularly ask for input on how to accomplish their goals during team meetings and one-on-one meetings.

The strategy here is to (1) normalize conversations on "Here's what I'm doing" and "How can you help me do it better?" and (2) drive a sense that we are all in this together, and all are willing to help each other get over the line. The following are a few examples of what that looks like.

Warren works for ECFA, which consistently wins the highest marks from the Best Christian Workplaces Institute. He is a member of the senior leadership team. As a team they frame three-year goals for the twenty-five-person staff, which the ECFA board then reviews and approves. Those goals are posted prominently in both staff meeting rooms. The current year's goals are also broken into quarterly goals, tailored to each team. Each person in the organization, including Warren, then has individual performance goals, either for six-week periods or quarterly. Warren's team regularly shares progress on their goals with each other for discussion, feedback, and encouragement. Warren also meets regularly one-on-one with the president/CEO to discuss challenges and questions about the goals, and for Warren to receive coaching and help toward achieving them.

Every quarter Léonce and his team go through three exercises: setting goals for the upcoming quarter, reviewing results from goals of the previous quarter, and contextualizing quarterly goals in light of annual goals.

In the middle of quarter two, for example, they begin to use either part of or an entire team meeting for each person to develop quarterly goals for their spheres of leadership and responsibility. Each person's goals are then weighed and measured against the overall organizational goals for that quarter, and then they're massaged by the team until they show the greatest prospect of producing results.

For another example, Léonce set a goal for the church to grow weekend service attendance by 25 percent. Once he presented this goal, Renovation's small groups pastor asked, "How many group leaders and groups will we need to facilitate this goal?" His question led to a robust discussion and adjustment to Léonce's goal. Had they not done this as a team, it could have meant a miss for weekend services and small groups, and it would have left a gap in answering why the goals were not achieved.

Finally—in a completely different context—Ryan remembers a high school basketball practice when the ticket to a water break came from completing a set of line-to-line runs within a given time. As a freshman Ryan was the last leg for his team and didn't make it over the line in time despite the cheers of his teammates. So they had to do it again, but faster. This second time Ryan's teammates decided to offer him a bit more enthusiastic cheering, even coming toward the midcourt line to entice his legs to push faster and get to that break. But still, he was too slow. Another run. This time, two junior teammates met Ryan at the far end of the court to accompany him for his last long run. One grabbed the front of his shirt and the other pushed him from behind as Ryan tried to just keep his legs under him. Water at last!

This is what great teams do. They help each other cross the line on both individual and team goals. One of the greatest indicators of a true team is the practice of mutual accountability—where everyone on the team holds everyone else accountable.[10]

STEP 34: SCHEDULE AFTER-ACTION REVIEWS (AAR) FOR EVENTS AND PROJECTS

Have you ever heard of a *hot wash*? A hot wash is the immediate after-action discussions and evaluations of a government agency's performance following a major event, training exercise, or similar session. The primary purpose of a hot wash session is to identify the strengths and weaknesses of the response to a given event, which then lends itself to another phase known as *lessons learned*.

If you do not evaluate, you will not make progress.

Hot washes are intended to guide future responses and minimize the potentiality of repeating errors, breakdowns in communication, or poor execution. A hot wash normally includes all the parties that participated in the exercise or response activities and results in a future improvement plan. When done effectively, it both benefits from and promotes psychological safety.[11]

After every event or project, your team should do the same, an after-action review (AAR). During an AAR, ask these five questions:

1. What were our desired outcomes? (goals)

2. What were the actual outcomes? (reality)

3. What went well? (wins)

4. What was unclear or confusing? (questions)

5. What can we do better? (growth opportunities)

By taking the time to analyze every nuance of an event or project—at a minimum— through these five questions, you position your team to avoid repeating errors, improve on execution, and guide future planning through past learning. The importance of this cannot be overstated—if you do not evaluate, you will not make progress.

NOW IT'S YOUR TURN

As you conduct your after-action reviews (see **Exercise 7.3**), don't fear failure. The best teams fail often but learn from those failures, getting better with each one. Or better, just replace the word *failure* in your entire vocabulary with *learning opportunity*. Remember that when Thomas Edison's team was working to invent the light bulb, they didn't fail once in their thousands of initial tries. Rather, they had thousands of learning opportunities, each moving them that much closer to success!

··

EXERCISE 7.3—Leading an after-action review

In your next team meeting, on a whiteboard or a piece of paper, write as the heading the name of the last event or project executed. Then answer these five questions pertaining to that project.

1. What were our desired outcomes? (goals)

2. What were the actual outcomes? (reality)

3. What went well? (wins)

4. What was unclear or confusing? (questions)

5. What can we do better? (growth opportunities)

Whenever you honestly and candidly engage in conversations like after-action reviews, discussions about team goals, and discussions about each other's individual goals, conflict will occur.

Of course, task-related conflict is essential for optimal team performance, and that's why we've encouraged you throughout this forty-step journey to regularly clash with one another, offering new ideas, articulating arguments, inviting feedback, pushing back on suggestions, and engaging with one another with radical candor. But occasionally that task-related conflict (an essential element of thriving teams) spills over into interpersonal conflict, where team members are at odds with one another.

To harness the power of task-related conflict while mitigating the harmful effects of interpersonal conflict, we encourage you to

- *Avoid making things personal or taking things personally.* This applies to the give and the take. When critiquing plans, keep it about the task, project, and so on, and don't take it to the next step by inferring, for instance, that your teammate always thinks in a certain way. And when receiving feedback, do all you can to focus on the issue, not your personality!

- *Address interpersonal conflict immediately.* Don't sweep it under the rug or pray that it goes away. Instead, engage it, bring people together, and talk it out.

- *Go below the surface when addressing hurts.* Conflict often erupts when hurt, anger, and frustration have been building. Dig in to the roots and causes of that pain to pursue healing and reconciliation.

- *Pursue fresh starts.* Do not let meeting frustrations linger. Let it go. Push for a relational reset, and model the power of the gospel as you seek and accept forgiveness and press forward in relationship and ministry together.

STEP 35: CONDUCT REGULAR SYSTEMS HEALTH CHECKS

Like the human body, every organization is an interconnected network of interdependent systems. In the body those primary systems include the respiratory, nervous, digestive, muscular, skeletal, reproductive, and circulatory systems. Each system plays a critical role in the overall health and function of the body, and within each of these systems are subsystems that also have significant roles.

Similarly, every organization is an interconnected network of interdependent systems. Though these systems are either strategically designed and ordered or incidentally and reactively created, they do exist, and if one of these systems fails, eventually the entire organization will begin to experience total system failure.

Thus, regular systems health checks are *critical* to the health and longevity of an organization. To do a regular health check you first have to know what the systems are in your organization. Léonce provides an example of Renovation Church's systems in figure 7.1.

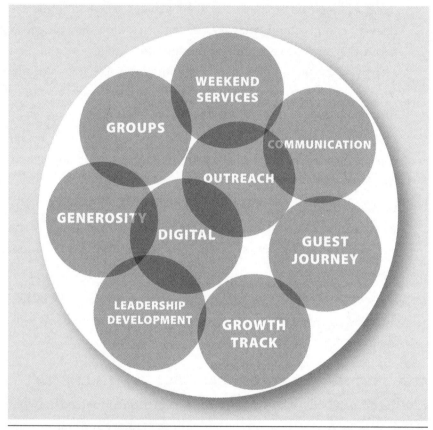

Figure 7.1. Unique systems of your organization

As with the systems of the body, each of these systems has subsystems, or subfunctions, that are unique and need monitoring, tweaking, tuning, and care. If you do not know the systems of your organization, your first step is to identify them as a team, name them, and order them. Once you have identified the unique systems of your organization, schedule at minimum a quarterly meeting in which you spend intentional time walking through each system, evaluating its health, and determining needed tweaking, tuning, or care.

■ ■ ■

Well done! You've taken serious steps to make measurement both meaningful and manageable. And now you're ready for the final movement—to reproduce your impact.

END-OF-CHAPTER SUMMARY AND ACTION ITEMS

If you forget everything else, remember this as you make assessments meaningful and manageable:

1. Set a few key team goals that will focus and energize your team over the next quarter.

2. Put a limit on what you measure so you don't overwhelm yourself or your team.

3. Cultivate mutual accountability, even developing individual performance objectives to increase buy-in and teamwork.

4. Engage in regular after-action reviews for your important projects, events, and initiatives.

5. Frequently conduct basic checks on all your vital organizational systems so you can make timely adjustments to optimize performance.

Reflection and Discussion Questions

1. What was the most useful or helpful insight you read in this movement?

2. How has your team typically considered the importance and practice of assessment, and how does this chapter support or challenge those views?

3. In terms of goal setting and measurement, what struggles has your team encountered (too few goals, too many goals, measuring the wrong things, etc.)?

4. At this moment, what opportunities do you see to engage in more meaningful and manageable assessments as a team?

5. What did each of you do or learn this week that will be most useful to this team?

Take It Deeper

1. Do some inventory of your sphere of leadership in the organization. Are you measuring too much? Are you measuring enough?

2. Explore your thoughts and feelings about inviting your teammates into your performance objectives. Is there any fear or pride that makes you uneasy about feedback?

3. Quiz yourself. Are you familiar with all your organization's key systems? If not, what are you going to do to learn them?

4. Move on to the next step, carrying with you the action steps you identified this week.

REPRODUCE YOUR IMPACT (STEPS 36-40)

YOU (AND YOUR TEAM)
HAVE MORE IN YOU THAN
YOU REALIZE

CONGRATULATIONS! Having already covered thirty-five steps, your team is likely already healthier than most. Therefore, what you've learned and internalized with your team is ready to go to the streets. If you're one step ahead of someone else, then you have something to offer. This chapter will help you take what you've learned and share it for cascading impact as you identify, recognize, and promote valued potential team leaders, take on new challenges with your team, and teach what you've learned to others—while driving it even further into your knowledge.

One of the biggest leadership stories of the last twenty years is leadership *development*.

Both in the church and the marketplace many great tools have developed that speak to both the why and how of reproducing yourself.

You've heard teachings on verses like "Follow my example, as I follow the example of Christ" (1 Corinthians 11:1 NIV), "What you have learned and received and heard and seen in me—practice these things" (Philippians 4:9), and "The things you have heard me say in the presence of many witnesses entrust to reliable people who will also be qualified to teach others" (2 Timothy 2:2 NIV).

In short, we know you've heard the message that you have something to model and teach to others. This chapter shows *how* you can reproduce the development you've experienced over this journey and share what you have learned and who you have become as a team with others.

STEP 36: ADOPT A KINGDOM MINDSET

"I need to resign from the team. I've been offered a new position at a similar organization across town. After praying hard, we're convinced it's a great opportunity for our family and for me."

> *When we adopt a kingdom mindset, we focus less on our little part and more on the King's mission across his realm.*

How would you respond if your best team member came in and told you this? Would you celebrate God moving your teammate to a place of greater kingdom use and impact? Or would you try to hold on as long as possible, afraid of losing this person's influence and good work on your team?

Though many wish the response would be the former, too often we find it hard to bless others because of the loss it means for those left behind. But when we adopt a kingdom mindset, we focus less on our little part and more on the King's mission across his realm. You hold on to people and programs with a bit less intensity.

You will be able to take the steps outlined in the rest of this chapter only if you first adopt an openhanded kingdom perspective. This means you truly wish to share with others the good things you've experienced and even—if necessary—the good people you've assembled in your team.

NOW IT'S YOUR TURN

Before you go further, use the exercise in **Exercise 8.1** to consider what it means for your team to take a kingdom mindset.

• •

EXERCISE 8.1—Identifying what your team can share with others

1. What does your team possess that you can share with others?

2. Which of your strongest team members are ready to offer their gifts and experiences to another team (such as to consult or facilitate)?

3. What principles you and your team have learned or processes you've mastered should be shared with others within your organization?

STEP 37: TAP SOMEONE ON THE SHOULDER TO MENTOR

Little compares to being tapped on the shoulder and then invested in by a respected leader. Each of us has been deeply influenced by a leader who saw something in us and invested themselves and their learnings. Ryan vividly remembers the day one of his college professors asked him to serve as a teaching assistant and participate with him in teaching a class. That simple act launched Ryan's teaching career, even though it took several years for it to fully unfold.

Of all the stories Warren has captured and told in the books he's coauthored, one that challenged him most personally is in the opening pages of *Hero Maker*. It describes Barry, someone who had accomplished much in life, far more than most, but still felt he was missing something. Then a friend challenged Barry to focus less on what *he* could personally accomplish and more on the leadership of *others*. Barry decided to make it his mission to change the trajectory of the lives of ten young leaders. When interviewed for *Hero Maker*, Barry had already found seven of them. Inspired, Warren decided to do likewise, intentionally tapping others on the shoulder and mentoring them.

Like his colleagues, Léonce, too, had his life forever changed by someone seeing the potential in him and tapping him on the shoulder. His former pastor in Oklahoma grabbed him one evening after the college ministry gathering and said very plainly, "God has a call on your life, and I am going to draw it out." While still a college student, within a year of that conversation Léonce was regularly preaching for both the college gathering and some Sunday mornings. Though Léonce had many other vying ambitions at the time, that moment set the trajectory of his life's work.

Who are you going to invest in? Take some time to discuss as a team who each team member might consider investing in to help them grow in their leadership. These could be people on your team or people on other teams in your organization. They might be people who have not stepped forward to engage or volunteer but are full of untapped potential. Especially if you are the formal team leader, consider that who you invest in might someday take your place. You might also consider people who are leading other teams but struggling with some of the issues your team faces or once faced.

NOW IT'S YOUR TURN

Use **Exercise 8.2** to identify at least *one* person each team member can invest in during the next season. (By the way, some teams we know require each team member to constantly be developing at least *five* people.) Then, take the steps to connect and begin to invest.

EXERCISE 8.2—Identifying leaders and teams to put your arm around

Go around your room (or Zoom panels!) and ask each team member to comment on question 1 and then after everyone responds, move to question 2 and determine next steps. Finally, be sure to check in on progress in one of your next team meetings, continuing to press forward.

1. Who would you like to invest in over the next few months? For each person you identify, what do you see in them, and why are you drawn to engaging with them?

2. How are you going to connect with the person you identified and by when?

STEP 38: ALWAYS DEVELOPING, ALWAYS INVESTING, ALWAYS REPRODUCING

"A-B-D" he said to Léonce between bites of grits and eggs. "ABD?" Léonce replied, with a puzzled look on his face. "Yes!" He responded, "A-B-D is Always Be Developing!"

Léonce shares this story as a key moment in his life and leadership. Because of his early breakfast with one of his mentors, this three-letter acronym would form a great takeaway that has

> *Always be developing yourself, and always be developing others.*

shaped some part of every facet of his team's development culture, including the rule of five—always have five people in your development cue or on your radar.

Always be developing yourself, and always be developing others.

If your organization is going to thrive, if it is going to fulfill its purpose, if it is going to be resilient in any respect, then a dogged determination to constantly be developing in every direction is critical.

We can guess what you are thinking, with everything else you have going on, being dogged about development feels impossible. But we boldly respond that *not* being so is the actual impossibility.

Making space to develop others is often easier than you think. It's often caught more than taught, mostly by being together and being intentional in what you do when you're together (and in assignments in between your hangouts). For example, over the next three months what would happen if you made a 5 percent adjustment in your schedule to nudge upward in practicing one or more of the following?

- *Work alone less frequently.* Recruit a partner or two for the various initiatives and projects on your plate. Some colleagues will just watch (and learn), some will help (and learn more), and some can take the lead in portions (and learn even more).

- *Bring others along as you lead.* Don't underestimate the impact of hallway conversations as you walk or commute to various responsibilities, intentionally having someone shadow you.

- *Don't take on too much yourself.* Leave room for others to contribute at a high level. Simply position yourself as a learner by asking questions like "What do you think I should do next?" or "Next time, how could I do this with greater impact?" Remember, you don't have to follow the advice! But feedback like this often makes for great discussion and learning moments.

- *Recognize your weaknesses and limitations.* While you don't want to focus too much on your weaknesses, scheduling time to shore up these areas will keep you constantly improving.

- *Ask people what they want to learn from you.* This might seem awkward, scary, or even presumptuous on your part. Maybe even frame the question with words like "As we spend time together, what's something over the next two or three times we're together that you'd like to ask me about or learn from me, especially regarding my experiences with teamwork?" Defining and mutually agreeing on a goal is usually the lion's share of framing a vibrant mentoring relationship.

STEP 39: DEVELOP A LEADERSHIP PIPELINE TO PREPARE NEW LEADERS ON YOUR TEAM

The best time to think about replacing your teammates is now, while they are still here and you don't have any glaring holes. Remind yourself that every person on this team is, in a sense, interim and will one day need a successor.[1] Ask yourself, What are you doing now to prepare for the inevitability of people transitioning from your team?

It's time to design a leadership pipeline (or pathway) that can help you plan for succession as your team membership shifts. Here's how:

1. Remember when you defined *leadership* (see step 26)? Place that as the goal for your leadership pipeline, that the people you develop will exhibit in their person and work your definition of a leader.

2. Review each role on your team and ensure that each is clearly defined multidirectionally in your organization, meaning you know how each role relates to the other roles. Who do they report to? Who is a peer? Who reports to them or you?

3. Curate the learning materials and cultivate the learning environment through which development will take place. Will you use cohorts primarily? Will there be a great deal of reading? Lectures? One-to-one investment? Labs and execution opportunities?

4. Go back to the list of "what you'll look for when adding team members" (step 14) and consider where those skills, attributes, and perspectives are often found in your organization.

5. Recruit, recruit, recruit. Tap on shoulders and tap into potential. At all times you should have a list of at least five people you have your eye on.

6. Begin a time-determined development cycle.

7. Find opportunities for others to lead and serve in varying places within the organization based on their particular gifts, tools, and passions.

Some of you might be thinking, *This is impractical for us; people aren't sitting around waiting to be called up to our team.* And you're right—they aren't sitting around waiting. Most likely they are busy working in other areas, but you can still be thinking and planning how to engage them and develop them now so they can be more ready to step in and engage in other roles in the future.

Since every position and every role in every organization is interim, you must plan now for how you will be one day replaced.

STEP 40: TEACH OTHERS WHAT YOU'VE ALREADY LEARNED

"To teach is to learn twice," says a famous Japanese proverb. Teaching others what you have learned as a team not only requires your team to articulate what's different and how you've grown, which will cement your own team's learning, but also extends the impact of how you have grown as a team over the last forty steps.

So, on this fortieth step your task is to prepare to teach others something you've learned on your journey toward becoming an unbreakable team, a team that can face anything and keeps moving toward your mission. We're sure through this process you and your team took a punch in the gut, but you got back up and kept going.

NOW IT'S YOUR TURN

Take some time to share with others something you learned along the way (see **Exercise 8.3**).

EXERCISE 8.3—Developing a workshop to build resilient teams

Work together to answer these questions as a group, developing a set of lessons to teach others.

1. What is the most important lesson you have learned over the last forty steps? Individually take some time to review your notes throughout this book, and then discuss together as a team.

2. What were the aha moments or key turning points for your team's growth during this journey?

3. What other teams or people in your organization might benefit from learning about the things you've learned or the key moments in your team's growth?

4. Choose one team or group of people to share your learnings with, and then develop a twenty-minute mini-workshop to express what you have learned as a team. Then encourage the other team in their continued growth and development.

5. Do the workshop, and then conduct an after-action review on how it went as a team. (When you do the AAR, see if your team has cultivated the trust and candor to be completely honest with one another. If so, you're now much further on your journey to become a team that can face anything.

You've made it through these forty steps. Well done! But, of course, you are not done. Not now. Not ever. So, in the final movement, consider how you can continue growing and applying all you've learned through this journey.

END-OF-CHAPTER SUMMARY AND ACTION ITEMS

If you forget everything else, remember this as you reproduce your team's impact (and further develop your team in the process):

1. Adopt a kingdom mindset, actively looking for ways to share what you've gathered and what you've learned with others.

2. Intentionally identify and invest in others.

3. Live into the A-B-D mindset: always be developing self, and always be developing others.

4. Cultivate a leadership-development strategy and pipeline to prepare others for their future assignments (on your team or outside your team).

5. Share something you've learned with others (again and again).

Reflection and Discussion Questions

1. What was the most useful or helpful insight you read in this movement?

2. How has your team adopted a kingdom mindset in the recent past, generously sharing with others what you have? How does this chapter support or challenge how you have sought to reproduce your team's impact in the recent past?

3. Who are some people with great leadership potential and who are you keeping an eye on?

4. At this moment, what are you most excited to share with others outside of your team from this journey?

5. What did you do or learn this week that will be most useful to this team?

Take It Deeper

1. Consider to what extent you've lived from a kingdom perspective in the past when valued team members have moved to new assignments. Be honest with yourself and, if you are bold, with your teammates.

2. Schedule coffee or lunch with one or two of the people you identified in step 37. When you meet with them, let them know what you see in them and your desire to invest in them.

3. Consider how you could make a slight change to invest more into developing others, using the ideas in step 38 as a starting point.

4. Take time to read and discuss chapter nine of this book, including the appendix.

ANTICIPATE THE NEXT STEP AND BEYOND

EVEN AFTER FORTY STEPS, the journey isn't over. This chapter will cast a vision of what's to come for your team and how you can drive what you've learned deep into your team's and organization's culture, all while pursuing continual refinement and improvement as a team.

If you are lucky enough never to experience any sort of adversity, we won't know how resilient you are. It's only when you're faced with obstacles, stress, and other environmental threats that resilience, or the lack of it, emerges: Do you succumb, or do you surmount?"[1] So writes Maria Konnikova, author of an article titled "How People Learn to Become Resilient."

If you made it this far, you've overcome many adversities and obstacles on your journey to develop a healthier, more resilient team. Chances are you're better because of them. Working through obstacles almost always makes a team stronger.

Just like kids who grow up in difficult circumstances but overcome them to excel in life, resilience is the ingredient your team needs to excel in the face of adversity.[2]

Working through obstacles almost always makes a team stronger.

Kids that excel in being resilient weren't necessarily born on third base or with rich parents. The same goes for high-performance, thriving, resilient teams. They don't always result from people with stellar educations or great social connections. No, resilient teams come from any type of background or context. Yet they rise to the challenge and thrive, both in productivity and interpersonal strengths.

In this brief chapter, we want to help you take stock of where you've been, where you are now, and what you should do next to drive your learnings deep into your team's and organization's culture.

WHERE YOU'VE BEEN

As you've walked this journey of forty steps across eight movements, you've come a long way. You've learned a lot:

- You've sought God (steps 1–5) and rearticulated your team's purpose (steps 6–10).

- You've documented a team charter (step 12) and refreshed your team's composition (steps 13–15).

- You've built and shared *Team Member User Manuals* (step 20) and clarified your vision frame (step 7).

- You've created better meetings (steps 21–25) and learned to make better decisions as a team (step 24).

- You've defined what a leader is in your organization (steps 26–27) and taken steps to turn your team into a powerful leadership incubator (steps 28–30).

- You've engaged in critical conversations within your team (can you find any of our steps that haven't encouraged candor or better communication?) and taken steps to increase meaningful accountability within and beyond your team (steps 31–35).

- You've developed a leadership pipeline (step 39) and taught at least some of what you've learned (step 40).

Look at what you've done, and take some time to name it and celebrate it (see Exercise 9.1). Remember that what you've done is both significant and important because leading a team is hard work.

NOW IT'S YOUR TURN

Exercise 9.1 will help you celebrate your accomplishments.

. . . .

EXERCISE 9.1—Celebrating your accomplishments

1. As you look back on this journey, what's changed for the better on your team?

2. In what ways is your team now better positioned and equipped to move toward God's preferred future for your team?

Make it personal: Take some time to tell each person (1) how they have powerfully contributed to your journey to a resilient team, and (2) what you have seen in them over this journey that makes you proud to have them on your team?

WHERE ARE YOU NOW?

The reality is that team learning "occurs best in cycles, which may take months or minutes depending on the nature of the work."[3] That means that while you've grown a ton over the last many weeks, begin to prepare now for your next cycle of team learning. A resilient team is always learning, growing, and improving.

You have invested forty steps (or more) in gaining many new insights and skills, becoming a high-performing, thriving, and resilient team. Compared to when you started this journey, how have you experienced a notable change in each of the following areas?

> *A resilient team is always learning, growing, and improving.*

In terms of becoming a *high-performance team,*

- Can you articulate a 5C purpose for your team?
- Do you now have a clear sense of your short- and long-term goals?
- Have you accomplished important team goals over this forty-step journey?
- Is your team able to make and implement key decisions?
- Have you maintained cohesiveness even as you've engaged with candor?
- Are you holding better meetings?
- Are you getting your work done more effectively and efficiently?

Next, in terms of becoming a *thriving team,*

- Are you operating more in your strengths than your weaknesses?
- Do you know what makes your teammates contribute their best work?
- Are you excited to go to team meetings and gatherings, confident they'll be productive, and engage in matters of importance?
- Do you enjoy working together with your teammates?
- Are you personally flourishing in your work on the team?

Finally, in terms of becoming a *resilient team,*

- Have trust levels within your team noticeably increased?
- Has your team's capacity for excellent performance grown?

- Is your team operating with radical candor, engaging honestly with one another to produce and perform at the highest level?

- Does your team face and not avoid the brutal realities of the challenges in your context?

- Is your team poised and equipped to face anything that comes in the future?

Take some time to answer these questions, first individually and then as a team. Consider how your team is doing, and what's changed over the past forty steps.

WHAT'S NEXT?

But don't stop there. Move forward now. Here are a few ideas.

1. *Post your team charter where everyone on your team can see it.* If you haven't yet, complete and review your team charter (step 12). Capture many of your key decisions and learnings over the last few months, then post the results conspicuously so your team can see them. If you're together in an office, this might be in a conference room or shared office space. If you are meeting virtually, it might be on your Base Camp home page.

2. *Share your team charter with key constituents of your team.* Share it with those who report to your team members, your governing board, your supervisor, and the like. Just as making personal health goals public increases the chance you'll do the hard work to pursue them, sharing your team's commitments with others will help hold your feet to the fire.

3. *Tell each other how much you have grown individually and collectively.* Discuss how each team member has embraced change and growth and the difference that has made for your team. Talk about the ways your team has grown. Put similar conversations on your calendar; aim to review your team's growth and make tweaks at least once a quarter.

4. *Share your vision with others in your organization.* No matter the level or place your team serves within your organization or

whether you're operating in a church, nonprofit, or in the marketplace as a leader and leadership team, others look to and rely on your team. Host a stakeholder meeting of some kind, and share your vision. Tell your stakeholders what your team is doing and why, and invite them to give you feedback and support.

5. *Embrace constant disruption.* The inconvenient reality is that our society, churches, and nonprofits are not going back to the old sense of normal. The new normal will not be a new fixed way of doing things. Rather, we're discovering a world where unpredictability is the norm. The stability that many parts of the Western world have so enjoyed for the last four decades isn't normal. Indeed, from a historical perspective the relative stability that has offered so much predictability is now a rarity—just think of the do-this-and-you'll-get-that principles undergirding the church growth movement over the last few decades. As one anonymous commentator recently observed:

> Imagine you were born in 1900.
>
> On your 14th birthday, World War I starts and ends on your 18th birthday. Some 22 million people perished in that war. Later in the year, a Spanish Flu epidemic hits the planet and runs until your 20th birthday. 50 million people die from it in those two years. Yes, 50 million.
>
> On your 29th birthday, the Great Depression begins. Unemployment hits 25%, and the World GDP drops 27%. That runs until you are 33. The country nearly collapses along with the world economy.
>
> When you turn 39, World War II starts. You aren't even over the hill yet. And don't try to catch your breath. On your 41st birthday, the United States is fully pulled into WWII. Between your 39th and 45th birthday, 75 million people perish in the war.[4]

Compared to that child of 1900, virtually every reader of this book has been spoiled with extraordinary stability over the last few decades, but it's time to face the truth that we're entering an unknown future.

In his breakout book *Canoeing the Mountains: Christian Leadership in Uncharted Territory*, Tod Bolsinger recounts the remarkable story of Meriwether Lewis and William Clark, who were military strategists, waterway experts, and renowned explorers.[5]

As the narrative goes, generations of leading thinkers supported the idea that if one were to enter the mighty US river system in the Midwest, it could be traveled across the continent. Eventually, the Mississippi River led to the Missouri River, which would carry one's vessel out to the Pacific Ocean.

The world needs your resilient, unbreakable team.

Nations wagered their future and livelihood on this "knowledge," believing that if they could control this central waterway, they could control the continent. Among these global leaders was President Thomas Jefferson who, for many reasons, wanted control of the waterway. He sent Lewis and Clark on their expedition, counting on them to secure whatever he needed to leverage control.

The story, unfortunately, goes quite a bit differently. What the entire Western world believed to be true about the North American continent was not so. As Lewis and Clark arrived at the end of the Missouri River, what they found was not more water to navigate, but mountains to climb.

At that moment they had one of three choices as they faced the unknown: (1) try to use what they knew to canoe the side of a mountain, (2) cower in the face of the unknown and go back the way they came, or (3) be resilient and proceed into the unknown with little more than a gut instinct of what to do next and the skills they had acquired on the journey thus far.

History tells us that Lewis and Clark and their team chose the third option. Through many trials and tribulations, they carried on through the mountains, until they reached their destination. There were great losses on the journey but also great gains. Because they chose to resiliently enter the unknown, hundreds of years of thinking were overturned, and the truth about the shape of North America was discovered.

As a leader and leadership team you have no idea what trials and treasures await you as you continue to enter the unknown, but you do know that with each lesson applied and step taken, you and your team are better prepared to face anything that comes your way. You've developed the resilience factor.

We believe that God has great plans ahead for your team—and that there are world-changing implications for the next step you take.

So, we beg you: discern it. Then take it. *The world needs your resilient, unbreakable team.*

ACKNOWLEDGMENTS

"You *killed* my great idea."

"No, I said only that your idea needs help, and I tried to offer it."

The words we three authors used with each other were a bit stronger. But that's the kind of radical candor and risk of conflict we voiced as we rigorously edited each other's stories and ideas. In the process we learned much about working as a team. Through doing the work with a clear purpose and goal, we indeed moved toward becoming a high-trust, high-performance team. We also became a resilient team through unexpected life events along the way, including a serious car crash (rolling over five times), a significant job transition and a cross-country move, house sales and purchases, unexpected immediate-family deaths, and more. Much stood in the way of finishing this book, but God got us through.

Together we thank God for his clear leading in drawing us together, clarifying the focus of this book, drawing out the best in each of us, and creating something far better than any of us could have accomplished alone. And that's what happens in a true team!

We also want to thank all the people who have supported us, starting with our wives—Jill M. Hartwig, Breanna M. Crump, and Michelle C. Bird. Your support, interest, insight, grace, feedback, coaching, and joy enrich our lives beyond measure! We each love the genuine teamwork developed with you in our marriages, families, and ministries. Truly each couple is better together because of you!

We also greatly appreciate the support and space offered by our primary employers. Ryan thanks Colorado Christian University, where he served through June 2022, for providing such a strong laboratory to learn about teams, both through study and through practice, and Vanguard University, which has offered open-arm support for the book as it releases. Léonce thanks Renovation Church, which has likewise provided a powerful and instructive context for developing resilient teams as well as for hosting the three authors for site interviews as we met in person to work on the book. Finally, Warren thanks the Evangelical Council for Financial Accountability, which could not have been more supportive in allowing the flexibility to work on the book as well as an incredible model of so many staff teams forming and purposing to thrive through high impact and resilience. We also credit the tremendous administrative support we've received both personally and through our organizations.

Numerous people have helped us along the way, especially Sanonna Newburn, who provided great support through the writing and editing process, wading through hundreds of comments and edits, fixing dozens of endnote references, and improving the manuscript piece by piece.

We also thank many friends who read portions of the book and made helpful suggestions. They include (in alphabetical order) Gretchen Bennett, Michelle C. Bird, Nathan and Anna Bird, Nicole and Joe Chinnici, Matt Coleman, Stephen Coppenrath, Margie and Joe Florio, Ernest Grant II, Dr. Derwin Gray, Doug Nelms, Pastor Alvin Smith, and Jason Sniff. In addition, Doug Nelms developed our website (www.resiliencefactor.info) and contributed to our social media and marketing strategy.

We also thank the large support team at InterVarsity Press, who turned our dream into a reality.

Most of all, we thank you—the reader—for making this journey with us, praying that your team is both different and better because of your investment in the forty-step journey of *The Resilience Factor*.

RESOURCES TO HELP YOUR TEAM GROW

Check out our *The Resilience Factor* website (www.resiliencefactor.info) for additional resources to help you develop and optimize your resilient team.

Find these resources and more:

1. Downloadable team charter template

2. Downloadable *Team User Manual* template

3. Discussion and decision-making techniques and tools

4. Emerging tools developed by the author team

NOTES

FOREWORD

[1]"A Navy SEAL Explains 8 Secrets to Grit and Resilience," *Barking Up the Wrong Tree*, accessed September 7, 2019, www.bakadesuyo.com/2015/01/grit, cited in Tod Bolsinger, *Tempered Resilience: How Leaders are Formed in the Crucible of Change* (Downers Grove, IL: InterVarsity Press, 2020), 109.

[2]Andrew Zolli and Anne Marie Healy, *Resilience: Why Things Bounce Back* (New York: Free Press, 2012), 7.

INTRODUCTION: WHY YOU NEED THE RESILIENCE FACTOR

[1]For classic thinking on the differences between management and leadership, see J. P. Kotter, *A Force for Change: How Leadership Differs from Management* (New York: Free Press, 1990).

[2]See the *Christianity Today* podcast *The Rise and Fall of Mars Hill*, www.christianitytoday.com/ct/podcasts/rise-and-fall-of-mars-hill.

[3]Mark C. Crowley, "It's Not Just Money: This Is What's Still Driving the Great Resignation," *Fast Company*, March 5, 2022, www.fastcompany.com/90727646/its-not-just-money-this-is-whats-still-driving-the-great-resignation.

[4]See Derek Thompson, "The Great Resignation Is Accelerating," *Atlantic*, October 15, 2021, www.theatlantic.com/ideas/archive/2021/10/great-resignation-accelerating/620382.

[5]"The 'Great Resignation' in Perspective," *Monthly Labor Review*, July 2022, US Bureau of Labor of Statistics, www.bls.gov/opub/mlr/2022/article/the-great-resignation-in-perspective.htm.

[6]This phrase was popularized in Marshall Goldsmith, *What Got You Here Won't Get You There* (New York: Hachette, 2007).

[7]Amy C. Edmondson, *Teaming: How Organizations Learn, Innovate, and Compete in the Knowledge Economy* (San Francisco: Jossey-Bass, 2012), 74.

[8]Jon R. Katzenbach and Douglas K. Smith, *The Wisdom of Teams: Creating the High-Performance Organization* (New York: Harvard Business School, 1993), 4.

[9]Katzenbach and Smith, *Wisdom of Teams*, 45. This definition of team is in contrast to what researchers call a "working group"—something many people experience and mistakenly think is a team. As the authors explain, "Too often the choice between working

group and team is neither recognized nor consciously made. A basic distinction turns on performance. A working group relies primarily on the individual contributions of its members for group performance, whereas a team strives for a magnified impact that is incremental to what its members could achieve in their individual roles."

[10]Katzenbach and Smith, *Wisdom of Teams*, 12.

[11]For more on high-performance teams, see Susan A. Wheelan, Maria Åkerlund, and Christian Jacobsson, *Creating Effective Teams: A Guide for Members and Leaders*, 6th ed. (Thousand Oaks, CA: Sage, 2020).

[12]Wheelan, *Creating Effective Teams*, 14.

[13]The late Richard Hackman theorized that great teams consistently increase their capacity while accomplishing their immediate goals. See, for instance, his "What Makes for a Great Team," *Psychological Science Agenda*, June 2004, www.apa.org/science/about/psa/2004/06/hackman.

[14]Keith Ferrazzi, Mary-Clare Race, and Alex Vincent, "7 Strategies to Build a More Resilient Team," *Harvard Business Review*, January 21, 2021, https://hbr.org/2021/01/7-strategies-to-build-a-more-resilient-team.

[15]For a great resource on how teams develop over time, and how leaders and members can help them progress, see Wheelan, *Creating Effective Teams*.

MOVEMENT 1: PRAY AND ASSESS YOUR SITUATION (STEPS 1–5)

[1]Susan A. Wheelan, *Creating Effective Teams: A Guide for Members and Leaders* (Thousand Oaks, CA: Sage, 2013), 13-14.

[2]For instance, see Kim Scott, "Build Radically Candid Relationships," in *Radical Candor: Be a Kick-Ass Boss Without Losing Your Humanity* (New York: St. Martin's, 2019), 3-18.

[3]Amy Edmondson, "Psychological Safety and Learning Behavior in Work Teams," *Administrative Science Quarterly* 44, no. 2 (June 1999): 350, http://doi.org/10.2307/2666999.

[4]Adapted from Amy Edmondson, "Psychological Safety and Learning Behavior in Work Teams," *Administrative Science Quarterly* 44, no. 2 (June 1999): 382-83, http://doi.org/10.2307/2666999.

[5]Max DePree, *Leadership Is an Art* (New York: Currency, 2004), 11.

MOVEMENT 2: CLARIFY YOUR PURPOSE (STEPS 6–10)

[1]David Maraniss, *When Pride Still Mattered: A Life of Vincent Lombardi* (New York: Simon & Schuster, 2000), 279.

[2]Jon R. Katzenbach and Douglas K. Smith, *The Wisdom of Teams: Creating the High-Performance Organization* (New York: Harvard Business School, 1993), 162.

[3]For more insights about what teams fight for, see David Burkus, *Leading from Anywhere* (Boston: Mariner, 2021).

[4]Gill R. Hickman and Georgia J. Sorenson, *The Power of Invisible Leadership*, 2nd ed. (Los Angeles: Sage, 2013), 3.

[5]Simon Sinek, *Start with Why* (New York: Portfolio, 2011).

[6]This outline of the 5 Whys exercise is based on Jim Collins and Jerry Porras, "Building Your Company's Vision," *Harvard Business Review* (September-October 1996).

[7]Simon Sinek, "How Great Leaders Inspire Action," TED, September 2009, www.ted.com/talks/simon_sinek_how_great_leaders_inspire_action.

[8]Robert Frost, "Mending Wall," 1914, www.poetryfoundation.org/poems/44266/mending
-wall.

[9]"Vision frame" is championed and explained in Will Mancini and Warren Bird, *God Dreams: 12 Vision Templates for Finding and Focusing Your Future* (Nashville: B&H, 2016).

[10]Thanks to Aaron Brown, associate chair of the church and ministry leadership department at LBC/Capital.

[11]Ryan T. Hartwig and Warren Bird, *Teams That Thrive* (Downers Grove, IL: InterVarsity Press, 2015), 104.

[12]For a great summary of group development as it relates to team performance, see Susan A. Wheelan, *Creating Effective Teams: A Guide for Members and Leaders* (Thousand Oaks, CA: Sage, 2013). In addition see Ruth Wageman, Debra A. Nunes, James A. Burress, and J. Richard Hackman, *Senior Leadership Teams: What It Takes to Make Them Great* (Boston: Harvard Business School Publishing, 2008). This book explains the importance of focusing on performance over trust in initial group development.

MOVEMENT 3: GATHER AN ALL-STAR CAST (STEPS 11–15)

[1]For more information on these self-evaluations, visit "Clifton Strengths," Gallup.com, accessed October 6, 2022, https://store.gallup.com/c/en-us/cliftonstrengths; "MBTI Basics," Myers & Briggs Foundation, accessed October 6, 2022, www.myersbriggs.org/my-mbti-personality
-type/mbti-basics; and Tim Scudder, "SCI 2.0 Methodology and Meaning," CoreStrengths, accessed October 6, 2022, www.corestrengths.com/sdi-2-0-methodology-and-meaning.

[2]Amy C. Edmondson, *Teaming: How Organizations Learn, Innovate, and Compete in the Knowledge Economy* (San Francisco: Jossey-Bass, 2012), 285.

[3]See Dan Busby and John Pearson, "Annual Affirmation Statement," *Tools and Templates for Effective Board Governance* (Winchester, VA: ECFA Press, 2019), 231-42.

[4]See further discussion on ideal team size in Ryan T. Hartwig and Warren Bird, *Teams That Thrive* (Downers Grove, IL: InterVarsity Press, 2015).

[5]Susan A. Wheelan, *Creating Effective Teams: A Guide for Members and Leaders*, 6th ed. (Thousand Oaks, CA: Sage, 2013), 39.

MOVEMENT 4: GET TO WORK (STEPS 16–20)

[1]Faaiza Rashid, Amy C. Edmonson, and Herman B. Leonard, "Leadership Lessons from the Chilean Mine Rescue," *Harvard Business Review*, July-August 2013, https://hbr.org
/2013/07/leadership-lessons-from-the-chilean-mine-rescue.

[2]"2010 Copiapó Mining Accident," Wikipedia, last modified April 21, 2022, https://
en.wikipedia.org/wiki/2010_Copiapó_mining_accident.

[3]We think this approach stems from a misunderstanding of Patrick Lencioni's helpful triangle in the *Five Dysfunctions of a Team* (San Francisco: Jossey-Bass, 2002), which argues that vulnerability-based trust is the foundation for effective teamwork. Defining trust as "the confidence among team members that their peers' intentions are good, and that there is no reason to be protective or careful around the group," he argues that "teammates must get comfortable being vulnerable with one another."

[4]For a good summary on how and when trust develops in a team and the relationship of trust and work, see Susan A. Wheelan, *Creating Effective Teams: A Guide for Members and Leaders* (Thousand Oaks, CA: Sage, 2013).

[5]Amy C. Edmondson, *Teaming: How Organizations Learn, Innovate, and Compete in the Knowledge Economy* (San Francisco: Jossey-Bass, 2012).

[6]Jon R. Katzenbach and Douglas K. Smith, *The Wisdom of Teams: Creating the High-Performance Organization* (New York: Harvard Business School, 1993), 109.

[7]For a more detailed framework on how to develop a life map, see Robert Clinton et al., "Instructions for the 'Life Map' Exercise and Telling Your Story," Soul Care, accessed October 10, 2022, www.soulcare.net/resources/Life%20Mapping%20Exercise.pdf.

MOVEMENT 5: DESIGN KILLER MEETINGS (STEPS 21–25)

[1]Jon R. Katzenbach and Douglas K. Smith, *The Wisdom of Teams: Creating the High-Performance Organization* (New York: Harvard Business School, 1993), 15.

[2]If you want to see what your meetings would cost, and the impact of making some small adjustments to them (such as inviting fewer attendees, shortening meetings by 15 minutes, etc.), check out "Counting the Cost of Time Spent in Meetings," Lucid, accessed October 10, 2022, www.lucidmeetings.com/lucid/calculators/people.

[3]For good tips on how to run better meetings, see Seth Godin, "Making Meetings More Expensive," *Seth's Blog*, January 4, 2011, https://seths.blog/2011/01/making-meetings-more-expensive.

[4]For a scholarly review of decades of research on this approach, see Marc Orlitzky and Randy Y. Hirokawa, "To Err Is Human, to Correct for It Divine: A Meta-Analysis of Research Testing the Functional Theory of Group Decision-Making Effectiveness," Small Group Research 32 no.3 (June 2001): 313-41, https://doi.org/10.1177/104649640103200303.

[5]For a full description of this technique, as well as many other group facilitation techniques that can help you run better meetings, see Judith Kolb, *Small Group Facilitation* (Amherst, MA: HRD, 2011).

[6]For more detailed instructions on the lotus blossom technique or a host of other procedures for analysis, creativity, and making good decisions, see the MindTools website (mindtools.com) or the Creating Minds website (creatingminds.org). See also Kolb, *Small Group Facilitation*.

[7]We believe so much in helping teams run better meetings, make better decisions, and generate more innovative ideas that we've developed additional resources available at www.resiliencefactor.info.

MOVEMENT 6: SHARPEN YOUR TEAM (STEPS 26–30)

[1]To learn more about how Christians use the Enneagram, see Ian Morgan Cron and Suzanne Stabile, *The Road Back to You* (Downers Grove, IL: InterVarsity Press, 2016); and Todd A. Wilson's, *The Enneagram Goes to Church* (Downers Grove, IL: InterVarsity Press, 2021).

MOVEMENT 7: PURSUE MEANINGFUL ACCOUNTABILITY (STEPS 31–35)

[1]Much of the material in steps 31–33 is taken from Ryan T. Hartwig, "Goal Setting for Thriving Teams," *Influence*, January 3, 2017, https://influencemagazine.com/practice/goal-setting-for-teams, used with permission.

[2]Jon R. Katzenbach and Douglas K. Smith, *The Wisdom of Teams: Creating the High-Performance Organization* (New York: Harvard Business School, 1993), 45.

[3]Susan A. Wheelan, Creating *Effective Teams: A Guide for Members and Leaders*, 6th ed. (Thousand Oaks, CA: Sage, 2013), 34.

[4]Though ubiquitous now, SMART goals were first developed by George T. Doran, "There's a S.M.A.R.T. Way to Write Management's Goals and Objectives," *Management Review* (November 1981): 35-36.

[5]John Doerr, *Measure What Matters: How Google, Bono, and the Gates Foundation Rock the World with OKRs* (New York: Portfolio, 2017).

[6]For instance, see Edward Deci and Richard M. Ryan, "Facilitating Optimal Motivation and Psychological Well Being Across Life's Domains, *Canadian Psychology*" 49, no. 1 (2008): 14-23

[7]Chris McChesney, Sean Covey, and Jim Huling, *The 4 Disciplines of Execution: Achieving Your Wildly Important Goals* (New York: Free Press, 2012).

[8]Dave Ferguson and Warren Bird, *Hero Maker: Five Essential Practices for Leaders to Multiply Leaders* (Grand Rapids, MI: Zondervan, 2018).

[9]David Burkus, *Leading from Anywhere* (Boston: Mariner, 2021), 141.

[10]Katzenbach and Smith, *Wisdom of Teams*.

[11]Amy C. Edmondson has written extensively about how destigmatizing failure by reflecting productively on it both results from and drives psychological safety. See Amy C. Edmondson, *The Fearless Organization: Creating Psychological Safety in the Workplace for Learning, Innovation, and Growth* (Hoboken, NJ: John Wiley, 2019), and *Teaming: How Organizations Learn, Innovate, and Compete in the Knowledge Economy* (San Francisco: Jossey-Bass, 2012).

MOVEMENT 8: REPRODUCE YOUR IMPACT (STEPS 36–40)

[1]The idea behind this statement is from the opening sentence in the first chapter of William Vanderbloemen and Warren Bird, *Next: Pastoral Succession That Works*, expanded and updated ed. (Grand Rapids, MI: Baker, 2020).

AFTERWORD: ANTICIPATE THE NEXT STEP AND BEYOND

[1]Maria Konnikova, "How People Learn to Become Resilient," *New Yorker*, April 11, 2016, www.newyorker.com/science/maria-konnikova/the-secret-formula-for-resilience.

[2]For a fascinating article based on resilience in children, see Konnikova, "How People Learn to Become Resilient."

[3]Amy C. Edmondson, *Teaming: How Organizations Learn, Innovate, and Compete in the Knowledge Economy* (San Francisco: Jossey-Bass, 2012), 241.

[4]"Is It Really That Bad? A Viral Social Media Post Puts Coronavirus Pandemic into Perspective," *Geo News*, May 6, 2020, www.geo.tv/latest/286677-is-it-really-that-bad-a-viral-social-media-post-puts-coronavirus-pandemic-into-perspective.

[5]Tod Bolsinger, *Canoeing the Mountains: Christian Leadership in Uncharted Territory* (Downers Grove, IL: InterVarsity Press, 2018).

REFERENCES

RECOMMENDATIONS FOR

FURTHER INSIGHT

BOOKS

Bolsinger, Tod. *Canoeing the Mountains: Christian Leadership in Uncharted Territory*. Downers Grove, IL: InterVarsity Press, 2018.

Burkus, David. *Leading from Anywhere*. Boston: Mariner, 2021.

Busby, Dan, and John Pearson. "Annual Affirmation Statement," *Tools and Templates for Effective Board Governance*. Winchester, VA: ECFA Press, 2019.

Cron, Ian Morgan, and Suzanne Stabile. *The Road Back to You*. Downers Grove, IL: InterVarsity Press, 2016.

DePree, Max. *Leadership Is an Art*. New York: Currency, 2004.

Doerr, John. *Measure What Matters: How Google, Bono, and the Gates Foundation Rock the World with OKRs*. New York: Portfolio, 2017.

Edmondson, Amy C. *The Fearless Organization: Creating Psychological Safety in the Workplace for Learning, Innovation, and Growth*. Hoboken, NJ: John Wiley, 2019.

———. *Teaming: How Organizations Learn, Innovate, and Compete in the Knowledge Economy*. San Francisco: Jossey-Bass, 2012.

Ferguson, Dave, and Warren Bird. *Hero Maker: Five Essential Practices for Leaders to Multiply Leaders*. Grand Rapids, MI: Zondervan, 2018.

Goldsmith, Marshall. *What Got You Here Won't Get You There*. New York: Hachette, 2007.

Hartwig, Ryan T., and Warren Bird. *Teams That Thrive*. Downers Grove, IL: InterVarsity Press, 2015).

Hickman, Gill R., and Georgia J. Sorenson. *The Power of Invisible Leadership*. 2nd ed. Los Angeles: Sage, 2013.

Katzenbach, Jon R., and Douglas K. Smith. *The Wisdom of Teams: Creating the High-Performance Organization*. New York: Harvard Business School, 1993.

Kolb, Judith. *Small Group Facilitation*. Amherst, MA: HRD, 2011.

Kotter, John P. *A Force for Change: How Leadership Differs from Management*. New York: Free Press, 1990.

Lencioni, Patrick. *Five Dysfunctions of a Team*. San Francisco: Jossey-Bass, 2002.

Maraniss, David. *When Pride Still Mattered: A Life of Vincent Lombardi*. New York: Simon & Schuster, 2000.

McChesney, Chris, Sean Covey, and Jim Huling. *The 4 Disciplines of Execution: Achieving Your Wildly Important Goals*. New York: Free Press, 2012.

Scott, Kim. *Radical Candor: Be a Kick-Ass Boss Without Losing Your Humanity*. New York: St. Martin's, 2019.

Sinek, Simon. *Start with Why*. New York: Portfolio, 2011.

Vanderbloemen, William, and Warren Bird. *Next: Pastoral Succession That Works*. Expanded and updated ed. Grand Rapids, MI: Baker, 2020.

Wageman, Ruth, Debra A. Nunes, James A. Burress, and J. Richard Hackman, *Senior Leadership Teams: What It Takes to Make Them Great*. Boston: Harvard Business School Publishing, 2008.

Wheelan, Susan A., Maria Åkerlund, and Christian Jacobsson. *Creating Effective Teams: A Guide for Members and Leaders*. 6th ed. Thousand Oaks, CA: Sage, 2020.

Wilson, Todd A. *The Enneagram Goes to Church*. Downers Grove, IL: InterVarsity Press, 2021.

ARTICLES

Clinton, Robert, et al. "Instructions for the 'Life Map' Exercise and Telling Your Story." Soul Care. Accessed October 10, 2022. www.soulcare.net/resources/Life%20Mapping%20Exercise.pdf.

Collins, Jim, and Jerry Porras. "Building Your Company's Vision." *Harvard Business Review*. September–October 1996.

"Counting the Cost of Time Spent in Meetings." Lucid. Accessed October 10, 2022. www.lucidmeetings.com/lucid/calculators/people.

Deci, Edward, and Richard M. Ryan. "Facilitating Optimal Motivation and Psychological Well Being Across Life's Domains." *Canadian Psychology* 49, no. 1 (2008): 14-23.

Edmondson, Amy C. "Psychological Safety and Learning Behavior in Work Teams." *Administrative Science Quarterly* 44, no. 2 (June 1999): 350. http://doi.org/10.2307/2666999.

Ferrazzi, Keith, Mary-Clare Race, and Alex Vincent. "7 Strategies to Build a More Resilient Team," *Harvard Business Review*. January 21, 2021. https://hbr.org/2021/01/7-strategies-to-build-a-more-resilient-team.

Godin, Seth. "Making Meetings More Expensive." *Seth's Blog*. January 4, 2011. https://seths.blog/2011/01/making-meetings-more-expensive.

Hackman, Richard. "What Makes for a Great Team." *Psychological Science Agenda*. June 2004, www.apa.org/science/about/psa/2004/06/hackman.

Konnikova, Maria. "How People Learn to Become Resilient." *New Yorker*. April 11, 2016. www.newyorker.com/science/maria-konnikova/the-secret-formula-for-resilience.

Rashid, Faaiza, Amy C. Edmonson, and Herman B. Leonard. "Leadership Lessons from the Chilean Mine Rescue." *Harvard Business Review*. July–August 2013. https://hbr.org/2013/07/leadership-lessons-from-the-chilean-mine-rescue.

Thompson, Derek. "The Great Resignation Is Accelerating." *The Atlantic*. October 15, 2021. www.theatlantic.com/ideas/archive/2021/10/great-resignation-accelerating/620382.

ABOUT THE AUTHORS

Ryan T. Hartwig, PhD (University of Colorado Boulder), is a higher education leader, communication professor, author, speaker, and consultant. Bringing a unique perspective as a teacher, researcher, and practitioner, he equips leadership teams and groups to thrive.

Ryan serves as provost and vice president of academic affairs at Vanguard University, Costa Mesa, California. For more than two decades he has taught courses in group, organizational, and leadership communication and has led, trained, and developed teams focusing on community development, discipleship, missions, leadership development, academic excellence, fundraising, and marketing in universities and churches.

Ryan has previously authored two books: *Teams That Thrive: Five Disciplines of Collaborative Church Leadership* with Warren Bird (Downers Grove, IL: InterVarsity Press, 2015), *Outreach* magazine's leadership resource of the year (2015), and *Leading Small Groups That Thrive: Five Shifts to Take Your Group to the Next Level* (Grand Rapids, MI: Zondervan, 2020).

Ryan frequently speaks to, trains, and consults with church and nonprofit leaders at numerous universities, churches, seminaries, and nonprofit organizations, and writes for practitioner-oriented publications.

Ryan and his wife, Jill, have four children: Halle, Alia, Katelyn, and Matthew.

Léonce B. Crump Jr. is an author, international speaker, and the founder and senior pastor of Renovation Church in Atlanta, Georgia. In 2008, Léonce and his wife, Breanna, answered God's call to relocate to Atlanta and begin the process of planting Renovation Church.

In his first book, *Renovate: Changing Who You Are by Loving Where You Are* (Colorado Spring, CO: Multnomah Books, 2016), Léonce details the obstacles he and his family faced and the revelations he uncovered during this process A champion for the church's participation in focused and intentional cultural renewal, Léonce is a leading voice of a generation committed to operating as God's redemptive agents in the earth. Ever the student, he is currently completing his doctoral studies.

Léonce's unique background includes experiences in the world of professional sports and the music industry. At the University of Oklahoma, Léonce was an all-American wrestler and defensive end for the Sooner football team; he went on to play professional football for the New Orleans Saints.

Léonce loves people and connects with the public through numerous podcasts, regular conference and church speaking, Twitter, Instagram, Facebook, LinkedIn, and his blog (www.leoncecrump.com).

Léonce and his wife, Breanna, reside in Atlanta with their three daughters and son.

Warren Bird, PhD (Fordham University), is senior vice president of research and equipping for Evangelical Council for Financial Accountability (ECFA), whose membership includes approximately three thousand senior leadership teams and more than twenty-five thousand board members, all representing the nation's best-known Christ-centered ministries and churches. Warren was previously director of research and intellectual capital development for Leadership Network, a nonprofit that helps leading innovative church leaders leverage their ideas for greater influence and impact. An ordained minister and staff pastor for fifteen years, he has also served since 1995 as teaching faculty at Alliance Theological Seminary in New York City.

Warren has coauthored thirty-three previous books, over two hundred magazine articles, and more than two dozen in-depth research reports. One of Warren's coauthored books won the prestigious Gold Medallion award from the Evangelical Press Association. Other awards include *Outreach* magazine's Leadership Resource of the Year (2015) for *Teams That Thrive*, coauthored with Ryan Hartwig.

Warren connects with the public through LinkedIn, Twitter, and ECFA's Large Church Trends blog (https:// largechurchtrends.blogspot.com).

Warren and his wife, Michelle, live in Metro New York City.

ALSO AVAILABLE

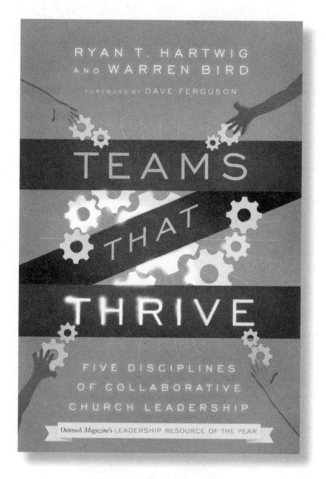

Teams That Thrive

978-0-8308-4119-6